MARIANNE FAITHFULL is a rock icon whose career has spanned four decades. Her landmark 1979 album, *Broken English*, is often cited as her definitive recording, and marked her arrival as one of the most original – and often controversial – singer-songwriters the UK has produced. Since then, she has released a number of albums, including *Rich Kid Blues*, *The Seven Deadly Sins*, *Vagabond Ways* and *Kissin' Time*, and has collaborated with the likes of Van Morrison, Jarvis Cocker, Damon Albarn and PJ Harvey.

Marianne has also won acclaim as an actress, having taken on roles including Ophelia in Tony Richardson's triumphant 1968 production of *Hamlet*, also starring Anthony Hopkins; Empress Maria-Theresa in Sofia Coppola's 2006 biopic *Marie-Antoinette*; and God in three episodes of *Absolutely Fabulous*. Most recently she starred in *Irina Palm*, which was presented at the Berlin International Film Festival 2007.

Visit her website at www.mariannefaithfull.org.uk

David Dalton, who worked with Marianne on this book, was initially a photographer, before becoming a founding editor of *Rolling Stone*. He is the author of some fifteen books: definitive biographies (*James Dean: The Mutant King*); stream-of-consciousness rants (*El Sid: St. Vicious*); on-the-road memoirs (*Piece of My Heart*); chronicles of the ghostly lives of others (*Faithfull* with Marianne); novels (*Been Here and Gone*); and articles on drugs, decadence and ontological drifters (*Mojo*, *Penthouse*, *Paris Match*, *Another Magazine*, *Gadfly*). His screenplay, *The Gospel According to Janis*, goes into production in 2008.

Also by Marianne Faithfull

Faithfull
(with David Dalton)

marianne faithfull

memories, dreams and reflections

with DAVID DALTON

HARPER PERENNIAL

London, New York, Toronto, Sydney and New Delhi

Harper Perennial
An imprint of HarperCollins*Publishers*
77–85 Fulham Palace Road, Hammersmith, London W6 8JB

www.harperperennial.co.uk
Visit our authors' blog at www.fifthestate.co.uk

This Harper Perennial edition published 2008
1

First published in Great Britain by Fourth Estate in 2007

A catalogue record for this book is available from the British Library

ISBN 978-0-00-724581-9

Set in PostScript Granjon by Rowland Phototypesetting Ltd, Bury St Edmunds, Suffolk

Printed and bound in Great Britain by Clays Ltd, St Ives plc

'F...   ...ineteen.

On holiday with Mick, the Summer of Love.

Maureen and Ringo Starr, George Harrison and Pattie Boyd,
with Brian Epstein impishly grinning in the background, 1966.
When the Beatles sang songs that made the world turn.

George on sitar,
Pattie on couch.

George and Pattie
at home in 1970.
They've just seen
god and would
like you to come
to tea.

The Rolling Stones Rock and Roll Circus, London, December 1968. Front row, left to right:
Pete Townshend, John Lennon, Yoko Ono, two little people, Brian Jones, Bill Wyman,
Eric Clapton, me, and that mad piano player. Second row (behind the little people):
Keith Richards, horse and cowboy, Mick and Charlie Watts.

For François

contents

List of Illustrations

All photos are from the author's private collection unless otherwise credited.

Me in the 1960s. Photo by Jean-Marie Perier, courtesy of Photos 12.

On holiday with Mick Jagger. Photo by John Kelly, courtesy of Camera Press London.

Maureen and Ringo Starr, George Harrison, Pattie Boyd and Brian Epstein. Photo by Bob Whitaker, courtesy of Camera Press London.

George and Pattie with a sitar. Photo by Thomas Picton, courtesy of Camera Press London.

George and Pattie at home. Photo by Christopher Simon Sykes, courtesy of Camera Press London.

The Rolling Stones Rock and Roll Circus. Photo by Mike Randolph, courtesy of Camera Press London.

In the studio with Mick. Photo by Gered Mankowitz.

Me in the 1970s. Photo by Ian Dickson / www.late20thcenturyboy.com

My grandmother holding my mother, Eva.

My mother dancing.

My mother holding me as a baby.

Me as a girl.

Girl in Bed, 1952 – Caroline Blackwood. Portrait by Lucian Freud.

Henrietta Moraes. Photo by Julian Lloyd.

Francis Bacon. Photo by Carlos Freire, courtesy of Photos 12.

The Jungman sisters, Teresa and Zita. Photo by Cecil Beaton, courtesy of Sotheby's.

Allen Ginsberg and Gregory Corso. Photo by Elsa Dorfman.

Bob Dylan and Allen Ginsberg. Photo by Elsa Dorfman.

A letter to me from my father.

Me with Nick Cave.

Me with Patrice Chéreau.

Writing songs with P. J. Harvey. Photos by Pierre Bailly.

On stage with Jarvis Cocker. Photo by Dave Bennett, courtesy of Getty Images Entertainment / Getty Images.

Me with my lead guitar player, Barry Reynolds.

My dear friends Perry and Sally Henzell.

My grandfather.

Me performing at the Pigalle in 2007, with Barry Reynolds. Photo by Dave Bennett, courtesy of Getty Images Entertainment / Getty Images.

The cast and crew from *Marie Antoinette* at Cannes in 2006. Photo by Benainous / Catarina / Legrand / Gamma, courtesy of Camera Press London.

acknowledgements

I would like to thank Deborah Theodore for allowing me to use excerpts from her Naropa diary; Hal Willner for sharing his memories of Gregory Corso; my inspired editor Louise Haines; J. B. Mondino; the noble Barry Reynolds; my beloved François Ravard – whose idea this book was – and the long-suffering David Dalton.

since writing my last book

Where to begin? Well, perhaps I should begin where I left off –
just about to start recording *The Seven Deadly Sins*. And around
that time I was, of course, also dealing with *the ramifications*. It's
weird the way people expect you to treat them in a book. I tried
to be honest but that didn't always suit everybody. A few people
were upset with what I'd said . . . usually about them. I guess I
was meant to say 'I owe everything to A_____' or 'Without
B_____ I'd never have . . .' Well, I'm sorry, but it wasn't that
kind of book. One thing I've learned from my last book is, it's
quite dangerous to summon up the past.

The one who really loved the book was Keith. Of course, he
and Dylan are the stars of the book, so no wonder. I was
puzzled when Bob mumbled that he didn't like it very much.

'Are you joking?' I said. 'You're the bloody, fucking *star* of the
book! Nitwit!'

Anyway, the fourteen years since *the book* have been, in many
ways, a very tough time. I've seen the death of a lot of good

friends. Denny Cordell and Tony Secunda, for instance, who both were responsible for getting me to write my first book, have passed on.

Denny's way of getting me to write the book was to give me Jenny Fabian's *Groupie*, a book I'd read already, actually. I just looked at it and said, 'Denny, no! No, it's not going to be like that. No way!' And it wasn't.

Denny was a legendary producer and A&R man. He produced Joe Cocker, the Moody Blues, Leon Russell, Tom Petty, Bob Marley, Toots, and many others. Denny's illness was terrible. He was ill for a long time. Denny got hepatitis C while working as a gofer for Chet Baker. He got into smack for one year but it eventually caught up with him.

I had a bout with hep C, too. I was shattered for a year, but by the time I got it they had somewhat perfected the treatment, using interferon and other drugs that weren't available when Denny got sick.

Tony Secunda's death came unexpectedly. Tony was the visionary agent of my autobiography and a wonderful madman manager of the old school. 'Sailor Sam', as McCartney calls him in 'Band on the Run', managed Procol Harum, the Move, T Rex, and me (briefly) with wicked provocation and panache. And a couple of years later Frankie (that mad girl he married) died, too, poor thing. There but for the grace of God, as they say! How I've made it this far myself, I have no idea. More of that later.

The saddest thing about getting old is the passing of your friends and lovers. Gene Pitney died. I liked Gene, he was a great shag and all that, but why did he die so young? He never drank or took a drug in his life. The odds of Gene dying in Cardiff – poor sod – are astronomical. I give him all honour and credit for the work he did, but what a place to shuffle off your mortal coil.

Then we began losing our parents. My father died in 1996 (my mother Eva had died in 1992). Keith's dad Bert, who I really loved, died recently and Mick's father just died, too – what a kind and gentle man he was. It was a serious moment for Mick. And I must say that both his mum and dad were really kind to me, and, well, let's just say I must have been a complete nightmare. I shudder to think. It wasn't as if Mick was this blameless soul exactly, but he wasn't like me, ever.

You start wondering about your own mortality when people begin putting you on the list of who's next in line. I remember going to David Litvinoff's funeral. Litz was a brilliant nutter, the catalyst for *Performance* and tutor in infamy to James Fox. Really the whole film is his style – allusive talk and gangster vibe. Lucian Freud painted a famous portrait of him called *The Procurer*. He was gay and didn't want to get old, so he killed himself. He committed suicide at Christopher Gibbs's house on the Aubusson carpet – Chrissy thought that was frightfully poor form.

I went to David Litvinoff's funeral with Christopher and Robert Fraser – a long time ago but it's something I'll never forget. We were in the limo having just come from the Jewish cemetery where we'd watched David's cremation – it was all very sombre – when Chrissy suddenly had a furious outburst. He looked at me and said: 'Well, I hope we never have to go through that again!'

————————————

People's idea of my social life is greatly exaggerated. I think they expect scandalous scenes with famous, outrageous people. You know, 'And then when Gore Vidal sat down with a line in front of him, he said to me . . .' and so on and so forth. Well, okay, I admit it's fun going to Sheryl Crow's Christmas party and seeing, I kid you not, Salman Rushdie talking to Heidi Fleiss, but for the most part my life isn't like that at all. Really. (You can believe me or not.)

Where was I? Oh yes, my lack of a social life. Well, it's true I have settled down just a bit. After I finished my autobiography I met François, while I was recording a song called 'La Femme Sans Haine'. Philippe Constantine, who invented world music for Richard Branson's Virgin Records, wanted me to do a duet with Ismaël Lô. Duets are something I never do, actually, but it turned out very well. Never got released, though, but I did meet François and fell in love.

Oscar Wilde's famous line, 'I can resist anything but temptation!', used to be my mantra, but, after a year and a half in which I've suffered the seven plagues of Egypt (and made four records and five movies), I've decided to modify my wilful approach to life. But first, let me tell you all about my wicked, wicked ways.

summoning up a sunny afternoon in the sixties (one of many)

Listening to *Revolver* always brings back memories of when we were all much younger and madder. Any excuse to get together, get high, get dressed up, or play each other our latest faves. In and out of each other's houses and at many different clubs, Pete Townshend and Eric Clapton dropping by Cheyne Walk, Mick and I visiting Brian Epstein; day trips to George Harrison and Pattie Boyd's multi-coloured hippie cottage, evenings at Paul McCartney and Jane Asher's.

Sometimes a tiny little moment, a gesture, will catch me unawares and transport me back to the sixties. One day I was waiting for a taxi after the Versace show, and suddenly there was Stella McCartney knocking on the window. As I turned and peered out, Stella gave me a wink and a thumbs up. And I had this sudden flashback to her dad, Paul, because that gesture and the wink is just what he used to do in those days. Kind of a corny music hall cheeky-chappie thing. So there was dear Stella by Starlight, who looks quite like the old man anyway, giving me Macca's sign!

The sixties was a great motley cast of characters in an ongoing operetta with multi-hued costumes to match. What I remember most is how beautiful everybody was, and, of course, the beautiful clothes: we dressed up like medieval damsels and princes, pirates, pre-Raphaelite Madonnas, popes, hussars, mad hatters and creatures visiting from other planets.

And then there were the courtiers and spear-carriers – all those strange characters around the Beatles and the Stones: the roadies, the hustlers, and instigators. George's personal assistant Terry Doran, the 'man in the motor trade', somehow getting hold of Lennon's psychedelic Rolls-Royce and ending up with a top job at Apple Corps. There was the sublime Derek Taylor, the Beatles' publicist and *agent provocateur*; the sinister Tom Keylock, Andrew Oldham's homicidal chauffeur; Brian's thuggish builder, Frank Thorogood, and his deathbed confession of how he murdered Brian Jones.

Then there were the Beatles' old roadies Neil Aspinall and Mal Evans. Big, benign, boyish Mal shot by the LA police during a misunderstanding. And Stu, Ian Stewart, the Stones' original piano player. I loved Stu! I remember for my twenty-first birthday Mick wanted to buy me a car and Stu was given the mission to find it. He turned up with the most beautiful car imaginable, a 1927 Cadillac, a Bonnie and Clyde car in an incredible beige colour with a red stripe across it where the doors opened. How cool was that? But despite Mick's efforts I never learned to drive. It was like driving a tank in the First World War, it had a gear stick and all that stuff, I could hardly see, my *nose* only just reached the windscreen.

Stu did me another great favour. Mick hated the Stones' performance in *The Rolling Stones' Rock and Roll Circus*. He just wanted the whole thing to go away. It was like the scene from *Snow White* where the Wicked Queen says to the huntsman: 'Go! Take her into the forest and destroy her!' with Mick as the Wicked Queen and Stu as the huntsman. Except that it wasn't me he was talking about, it was the cans of film of my part in *Rock and Roll Circus*. He wanted those tapes destroyed. Burned. Thrown into the Thames. For ever eliminated. And Stu said, 'Yeah, okay, Mick, will do.' But he *couldn't* do it! 'Where can I put these cans of film,' Stu thought to himself, 'where Mick will never think to ever look?' And so he took them to Eel Pie Island and said, 'I say, Pete [Townshend, this was], I've got these old cans of film. Do you mind if I leave them in your garage?' And Pete said, 'No, Stu, go on. That's fine, you know, I don't mind, don't use it, there's nothing really in there.' And there they lay, mouldering away, for twenty-five years, until one day, God knows, Pete, clearing out the garage, found the film and it said *Rock and Roll Circus* on it! And he goes, 'Oh, hey, what's this?' And being incredibly smart, he put it on his home projection and watched it, and every single shot was of me for the *Rock and Roll Circus*. He called Allen Klein and said, 'I've got something you'll be very interested in. I've found the lost Marianne film from the *Circus*. What do you want me to do with it, Allen?' And Allen said, 'Hallelujah! I'll send a courier.' And he did. He sent his daughter, Robin Klein, to pick it up. Townshend knew about this problem because of course The Who were very much involved with the *Rock and Roll Circus* – and he also knew that one of the reasons the show hadn't come out was because they appeared to have upstaged the Stones. They really didn't, but, anyway . . .

And there it all was, except for one really beautiful crane shot. I don't know what happened to that. Maybe Mick was so angry that he just had one roll of film out of a can, tore it into a million pieces and burned it in the back garden as he and Bianca danced around it hooting like owls!

I loved Mick, I really did, you know – but if I had stayed in that situation with Mick, all that money, going to the South of France, Keith and Anita Pallenberg, blah-di-blah, *Goat's Head Soup*, I'd be dead, and I knew that. And if I was going to go down, I wanted to go down my own way! Not with some adjunct decadent ringleader and his scurvy crew!

When I split with Mick and left with Nicholas, I took a beautiful Persian carpet and some Ossie Clark dresses and all my Deliss silk clothes. So these were the clothes I was wearing when I was living on the street, a wraith-like vision, an anorexic waif, feeling no pain, and not feeling any cold either, of course, you see, because of the smack.

At this point, I'm sort of an honorary Rolling Stone, a situation I'm a little ambivalent about. I love them and we had such great times, but it was a really hard scene to be in. I was never going to be good at functioning in that bitchy world, with all those betrayals. Now, when I go to see them backstage or at the George V Hotel, it's lovely to see Keith and Ronnie and Mick and Charlie. Charlie's always been a delight. I love to go and hear him outside of the Stones environment when he plays his jazz shows in London.

I'm still scared of the Stones because I always have this feeling – and it's not just an illusion – of being sucked in again. Unlike Anita, I don't have any immediate connection with them. I'm a free agent, and yet, when I see them, I suddenly feel drawn in. I go back to their very beginnings. I am part of them. I know that. And that's okay.

One of the favourite places Mick and I liked to hang out was George and Pattie Boyd's house in Weybridge. Mick loved George and I thought Pattie one of the most beautiful people ever. I loved the way she dressed, her fantastic sense of style. Psychedelic dresses in beautiful colours or little skirts that showed off her wonderful legs.

During those magical afternoons George would be the perfect host, serving up exotic teas, fat joints, and his new songs like exquisite delicacies offered for our consumption. A little bungalow (by rock star standards) brightly painted in sparkly psychedelic ice-cream colours, very warm and cosy and friendly, like the people who lived there, with a garden full of sunflowers and cushions outside. Just a very soft, gentle vibe, as if this fairy-tale cottage were conjured out of his sweet melancholy songs.

It was always far easier to go and visit people from other bands. You didn't have all the stresses and strains you do with your own group. At Redlands, Keith's house in West Sussex, there was always some tension – undercurrents that I couldn't even put into words. Subterranean stuff, which I think is always lurking about in any band. What makes an interesting band is that incongruous combination of people at odds. The tension makes for great music, but it doesn't always make for the easiest social situations.

Clearly there were similar issues with the Beatles, but any raging insecurities or problems within the group were never apparent at Weybridge on a sunny afternoon, with George sitting cross-legged on a kilim playing us his songs.

So being with George and Pattie was very relaxing. Mick and I were able to lie back on Moroccan cushions, get high and float away listening to George's new songs. When he wasn't playing his own stuff, he would be playing Ravi Shankar on those beautiful green discs we all used to have. I do think he very much brought all that into our world.

Mick loved George's songs – those wonderful songs on *Revolver* – but George never felt that anybody appreciated his songs, really, or thought they were as good as John and Paul's. George was racked with doubt about his work, but it's now obvious what a great songwriter he was. 'Beware of Darkness' is as good as anything anybody ever wrote.

In a way, Brian Jones was George's counterpart in the Stones. But there was a big difference in their personalities. The thing about George – and we all feel it strongly now that he's gone off and left us – is that he *plunged* into things. Whatever he got into, whether it was the sitar and Ravi Shankar or the Maharishi, he walked right in and never looked back, and that takes a lot of confidence. Brian, on the other hand, was all flash. He loved to astonish – and then on to the next thing. Sometimes I'd get the eerie feeling that – like the positive and negative in a photograph – George was the positive version of Brian. They were quite similar in many ways; both could play a lot of different instruments and were hugely talented. But of course one huge difference was that Brian was unable to write songs. His perpetual upsetness and unhappiness and paranoia and low self-esteem all worked against him. It was tragic because he wanted to be a songwriter more than anything. I've watched the painful process, Brian mumbling out a few words to a twelve-bar blues riff and then throwing his guitar down in frustration.

I think in Brian's state writing a song probably wasn't possible. He could only do it through another medium, through Keith. I guess the closest he came to it was 'Ruby Tuesday', where his melancholy recorder wistfully carries that sense of irretrievable loss. 'Ruby Tuesday' was a collaboration between Keith and Brian. It's one of the few cases where Mick had nothing to do with a Stones song, neither the lyrics nor the melody – but he and Keith got the writing credit. Without Brian, there wouldn't *be* a 'Ruby Tuesday'.

It's funny how each drummer was so perfect for the band they were in. Mick admired Ringo's drumming – it was so simple, so spare, so incredibly on the money – but it wouldn't have fitted into the Stones at all. You couldn't have taken Ringo and put him in the Stones; you couldn't have Charlie Watts drumming for the Beatles. As for Keith Moon, his drumming would have got too much in the way of the guitars and the vocals in either the Stones or the Beatles, but could there have been a more perfect drummer and maniac for The Who than Keith Moon?

I've heard this funny theory that Mick wanted to be a Beatle and that John wanted to be a Rolling Stone, but I think it misses the point by a mile. Mick loved the Beatles, of course, and obviously there was a bit of natural competition going on there, but I don't think that was unhealthy at all – they *sparked* off each other.

You know, people have said, with a little truth to it, that the Beatles were thugs pretending to be gentlemen, whereas the Stones were gentlemen *pretending* to be thugs, and this is where it all gets so interesting when we talk about the music, because you've got those contradictory aspects bleeding through. They're very subtle, but they're there, and that's what makes the music so compelling, the rent in the temple cloth.

The thing about the Stones is that they were very intense about everything: about writing, recording, and performing. The Beatles had a similar intensity in the studio, but they were never able to transmit that on to the stage. They were so unlucky with what they went through in the early days; not being able to hear themselves play. It was a complete fuck-up that we have to lay, I'm afraid, at Brian Epstein's door.

One of the things a manager must do is make sure that the technical aspects are taken care of when the musicians go on stage. Kit Lambert and Chris Stamp did it for The Who, Clapton's crew looked after Eric. The basic responsibility of people who take care of any band, including mine, is to make sure that the sound is right so that the musicians can enjoy the experience. That's vitally important, and Brian Epstein just didn't get that together. He never made that leap from playing small venues in the north of England to playing Shea Stadium. It's tragic to see the Beatles on stage with their tiny amps, unable to hear a thing. And naturally, after that last tour, they came back from all that and said, 'That's it! We're never going out again!' And then Brian Epstein got really depressed because he realised he was almost out of a job.

The Beatles completely evolved from the pop business. The Stones began as a Brit Chicago R & B group and then lurched into a more raunchy rig than the Beatles ever managed. When the Beatles stopped touring in 1966 they were still the lovable Fab Four – they were rock'n'roll muppets. The Stones were menacing and sexy. A lot of that had to do with the kind of music they played, with Andrew Oldham, their manager, pushing their bad-boy image and Mick and Keith's natural bolshiness. But much of it, too, had to do with Mick's savvy on the business side. They never had a manager in the sense of a daddy figure like Brian Epstein telling them what to do – Andrew was *younger* than they were *and* more reckless. They weren't dependent on Allen Klein or Andrew – they were their own gang. Also, you have to take into account that the Beatles were the pioneers and nobody had invented proper speakers yet. It was so early on that nothing had been sorted out yet.

Mick might, very occasionally, put the Beatles down for their provincialism, which, if you're from London and they're from Liverpool, is a very natural reaction. But he'd never put their music down. Well, of 'Yellow Submarine' or those whimsical Beatle songs he might say, 'Now that is a bit silly.' I never thought so; I loved it, still do. Also something like 'With a Little Help from My Friends', but these are obviously not the sort of things the Stones would be into.

Anyway, when you listen to the Beatles carefully, and the John Lennon stuff in particular, they aren't all sweetness and light. There's an edge to their music; there's a real soggy, dark, dirty bit in it that bleeds through. Their sweetness is very superficial. You hear the undercurrent in Paul's bass playing, you hear it in John's harmonies, you hear it in the call-and-response stuff. Maybe not the first couple of records, but when you get to *Revolver* and *Rubber Soul*, things begin to darken. And there's something very weird about *Sgt Pepper*, too. It's not at all what it appears to be. I've found subsequently that listening to *Sgt Pepper* can be a bit of an unsettling experience. *Pet Sounds* still comes across as very beatific, so innocent and yearning, whereas *Sgt Pepper* really doesn't.

Brian Epstein didn't seem to get it that one of his jobs was to make sure that his precious boys were happy onstage and could hear each other and that they weren't torn to pieces all the time by crazed fans. The most basic of needs, you know, just to make sure they weren't being hounded day and night by cameras and reporters, with absolutely *no* time to themselves. These awful things kept happening and he wasn't able to deal with them. That's one of the reasons why Derek Taylor, their publicist, was so handy, because he was such a gentleman, *and* a hipster plus he had that ability to make people snap to attention. Invaluable, since Brian Jones would go missing in the middle of tours, recording sessions, negotiations, and nobody could find him. Epstein was a handy front for the Beatles in the beginning, because he seemed to be a gentleman – in appearance he was upper middle class. At first he was able to keep that together and where he did fall short he wasn't that different from many of the early managers. It was new territory and they didn't know what the hell they were doing.

Brian Epstein was so talented and had so many gifts and yet in many ways it was as if he really wasn't paying attention. He fucked up. Beautifully. He was eaten up by what he called his 'problem'. This was all long before it was cool to be gay. He was wrestling with real demons there, boy, as much if not more than our Andrew. But the difference was that Andrew seemed to *enjoy* his demons, let's put it that way. Andrew embraced them, whereas poor Brian just beat himself into a bloody pulp over it. Nobody guessed that he was so terribly depressed and desperate. I had no clue anything was awry. The many times that I went down to see him in his lovely country house, they were beautiful idyllic afternoons. He seemed happy, and put up such a front you could never guess what was going on in the dark corners.

We talked and talked, about ballet, opera, the theatre. We talked about Margot Fonteyn and Nureyev, Vanessa Redgrave, Maggie Smith's production of *Miss Julie*. At that time Brian was agonising over *Up Against It,* the Joe Orton script that he wanted the Beatles to do. He was worried it was too far out.

'I don't know,' he said, flipping through the script. 'Some of it is extremely provocative and *nasty*.'

'C'mon, Brian,' I said. 'It's Joe Orton; they'll eat it up.'

'Well, the Archbishop of Canterbury turns out to be a woman, the boys get dressed up as women, commit adultery and murder, and are involved in the assassination of the Prime Minister. Do you really think audiences can stomach this stuff?'

'It's farce, Brian,' I told him. 'And, let's face it, at this point the Beatles could do with something edgy.'

I hadn't, of course, actually *read* it, and when I did, I saw how tricky – unfortunately – it would be for the Beatles (with the exception of John). There were wonderful outrageous lines. The Archbishop of Canterbury was pure hysterical camp: 'I'm Princess of the Church. Let me pass. I've some hard praying to do.' The Stones *maybe* could have got away with it, but for the Fab Four it would've been a bit of a stretch.

Orton rightly anticipated that it would be turned down. In his diary he wrote scathingly of Epstein: 'An amateur and a fool. He isn't equipped to judge the quality of a script. Probably he will never say "yes", equally hasn't the courage to say "no". A thoroughly weak, flaccid type.'

Too bad. I think if the Beatles had done Orton's script, it would have really helped Brian – moved him up a level. Although Joe Orton made an unfortunate choice in a lover (who killed him), his take on the Beatles was spot on. He had the right cheeky attitude to the whole thing, and he came from the same milieu as the Beatles. It would have been brilliant if they'd filmed Orton's script. Would have helped Brian exorcise some of his shit, too.

I know Brian Epstein really liked me because towards the end of one of these teas he asked me to marry him; not that he was exactly serious, but for a second I actually considered it. Come to think of it, I know *exactly* what stopped me. It was our Mick walking in and saying, 'Come on, darling, we've got to go home now.'

Kit Lambert, who along with Chris Stamp managed The Who, was a wonderful maniac. I remember in the early seventies visiting Kit in some really dreadful, scabby flat in Notting Hill, before Notting Hill became fashionable. It was a trip, I can tell you, both of us doing lots of heroin and coke and alcohol – Kit *loved* alcohol. We had a whale of a time as Kit regaled me with stories about his dad Constant Lambert, the composer, acting out scenes from operas, scenes with divas and soirées with princesses and rent boys.

I didn't know Kit in his heyday; I only got to know him on the way down, which was more interesting I think, because in an odd way that's when he was truly in his glory – he was a connoisseur of the lower depths, an area in which I am also somewhat of an expert. The only good thing you could say about Kit's self-demolition was that he had a perverse kind of pleasure in all of it. He was such a fascinating pervert with a classical education. He used to say things like, 'The destruction of Pompeii . . . one of the *most* magnificent events in history. Those two naked boys preserved *in flagrante delicto* for all eternity!'

Kit liked building things up, like a child with a sand castle, and then, oh, the mad joy of tearing them down. He enjoyed seeing everything in turmoil, going up in flames. Like Nero, Louis-Ferdinand Céline, and Pliny the Elder, he loved a great catastrophe – especially if he'd engineered it himself. He loved talking about his disasters – few understood that he relished them as perverse works of art.

I remember once he wanted to take me on a lig to the Cannes Film Festival on a yacht with lots of drugs. In spite of his fallen state he was always very posh. But I wasn't in any condition to go to some fancy international event and display myself in my wretched condition, so regretfully I declined. Thank God. I would have made the most awful fool of myself, and in public. I had been doing that far too much in front of people as it was – along the lines of the famous Mandrax head-in-the-soup incident. Kit went and made a fool of himself in the grand manner, but then he was a man for whom flamboyant bad behaviour was a fine art.

One of the curious things about Kit, of course, was that his father had been a great composer; and that leads us directly to *Tommy*, The Who's rock opera. You can see why Pete with his transcendent – and overweening – approach to rock would have been so receptive to Kit's idea, and I do think it was Kit's idea – writing a rock opera. After *Sgt Pepper* everybody wanted a crack at the rock *Gesamtkunstwerk*, but it was not on. The only person who managed anything like it, and, in fact, preceded it, was Brian Wilson with *Pet Sounds*. And it was *Pet Sounds* that helped give *Sgt Pepper* wings.

Kit came to a sad end, alas. He died of a cerebral haemorrhage after falling down the stairs of his mother's house in 1981.

———————————

Visits to Paul and Jane Asher weren't quite as relaxed as those Mick and I spent with George and Pattie. With hindsight I can see that they were rather uptight. There were constant little frictions. Mick and I were very close and we would never have done anything like fret about windows being open or closed, or anything as petty as that, but this is what happens when couples start to come apart. In any case I was in a very different position to the one Jane found herself in. I'd done what Paul wanted Jane to do, and given up my career. I wasn't going on tour with the Old Vic; I wasn't taking any more movie roles and very few parts in plays. I gave up everything I'd been doing, apart from a little bit of theatre.

Jane was a serious actress and wanted to continue her career, but Paul had other ideas. That's why Linda was so perfect for Paul; she was just what he wanted, an old-fashioned Liverpool wife who was completely devoted to her husband. In a way, that's what Mick wanted, too, and for a while I acquiesced, but in the end it kicked back very badly. On the other hand, Paul isn't exactly the regular bloke he appears. For one thing, he was always intellectually curious. Not only was he into electronic music and Stockhausen and all of that, but he was into Magritte, pop art, the Expressionists and even avant-garde theatre. I believe it was Paul who first thought of Joe Orton as the screenwriter for the next Beatles movie. He'd been to see *Loot*, Orton's outrageous phallic farce, and liked it. He encouraged Brian Epstein to arrange a meeting with Orton, and in Orton's diary he describes getting on famously with Paul.

Arrived in Belgravia at ten minutes to eight . . . I found Chapel Street easily. I didn't want to get there too early so I walked around for a while and came back through a nearby mews. When I got back to the house it was nearly eight o'clock. I rang the bell and an old man entered. He seemed surprised to see me. 'Is this Brian Epstein's house?' I said. 'Yes, sir,' he said, and led the way to the hall. I suddenly realised that the man was the butler. I've never seen one before . . . He took me into a room and said in a loud voice, 'Mr Orton.' Everybody looked up and stood to their feet. I was introduced to one or two people. And Paul McCartney. He was just as the photographs. Only he'd grown a moustache. His hair was shorter too. He was playing the latest Beatles record, 'Penny Lane'. I like it very much.

Then he played the other side – Strawberry something. I
didn't like this as much. We talked intermittently. Before
we went out to dinner we agreed to throw out the idea of
setting the film in the thirties. We went down to dinner.
The trusted old retainer – looking too much like a butler to
be good casting – busied himself in the corner. 'The only
thing I get from the theatre,' Paul M. said, 'is a sore arse.'
He said *Loot* was the only play he hadn't wanted to leave
before the end. 'I'd've liked a bit more,' he said. We talked
of the theatre. I said that compared with the pop-scene the
theatre was square. 'The theatre started going downhill
when Queen Victoria knighted Henry Irving,' I said. 'Too
fucking respectable.' We talked of drugs, of mushrooms
which give hallucinations – like LSD. 'The drug, not the
money,' I said. We talked of tattoos. And after one or two
veiled references, marijuana. I said I'd smoked it in
Morocco. The atmosphere relaxed a little. Dinner ended and
we went upstairs again. We watched a programme on TV;
it had phrases in it like 'the in crowd' and 'swinging
London'. There was a little scratching at the door. I thought
it was the old retainer, but someone got up to open the door
and about five very young and pretty boys trooped in. I
rather hoped this was the evening's entertainment. It wasn't,
though. It was a pop group called The Easybeats. I'd seen
them on TV. I liked them very much . . . A French
photographer arrived . . . He'd taken a set of new
photographs of The Beatles. They wanted one to use on the
record sleeve. Excellent photographs. The four Beatles look
different in their moustaches. Like anarchists in the early
years of the century. After a while . . . I talked to the

leading Easybeat. Feeling slightly like an Edwardian masher with a Gaiety girl. And then I came over tired and decided to go home. I had a last word with Paul M. 'Well,' I said, 'I'd like to do the film. There's only one thing we've got to fix up.' 'You mean the bread?' 'Yes.' We smiled and parted. I got a cab home. Told Kenneth about it. Then he got up to make a cup of tea. And we talked a little more. And went to sleep.

JOE ORTON and JOHN LAHR, The Orton Diaries

While Brian Epstein came off as a shadowy, pathetic character.

Somehow I'd expected something like Michael Codron. I'd imagined Epstein to be florid, Jewish, dark-haired and overbearing. Instead I was face to face with a mousey-haired, slight young man. Washed-out in a way. He had a suburban accent.

Mick was initially supportive of my acting, but I sensed it was something he'd rather I not do. I was the consort – my career would distract from the image he wanted to create. I had absolutely no wish to compete with him, but eventually I decided acting would be okay since it was far enough away from what he did. I thought it wouldn't affect him, but, fuck me, then he wanted to act, too! He can't help it; he's just got to compete.

I stopped working, but then other issues began to raise their ugly heads. The Devil, as we know, makes work for idle hands. I got heavily into drugs in spite of all the warnings, which, again, I can only see from a distance. The biggest warning of all should have been Brian's headlong plunge, but I didn't realise it, and by the time I did it was too late. I had my overdose in Australia, and that was the beginning of the end for Mick and me. It's easy enough, after all, to rationalise how other people's problems are different from our own, and honestly there was no logical reason why I would've compared my fate to Brian's.

Some very odd things happened to me in Australia when I OD'd on all those sleeping pills. It sounds strange, but I have a feeling that those six days out, unconscious, did some very bizarre things to me. I always thought that I came through that with no damage, but I know that when I had my biopsy last year the results showed very old scarring on my liver – apparently the 150 Tuinol and six days' unconsciousness caused serious liver damage. Other bizarre things happened. Before the OD I could speak French, and afterwards I couldn't. An entire language had somehow got lost.

I'm always amazed at how scenes from the past get congealed into rabid set pieces. There's the whole Redlands business. It's so complicated and has an endless life of its own. Almost immediately it became an emblematic part of Stones history, but my position was much dodgier – my role was ambivalent and eventually had disastrous effects on me and on my relationship with Mick. It was a horrible ordeal, but initially it created a bizarre bond between us. I took the poison-pen letters and all those dreadful things in the papers too hard. I was too young and insecure to have all that hatred directed at me and didn't know how to deal with it. I turned it all on myself.

Mick's attitude was much, much healthier. Like, 'Well, they're just idiots. I'm not gonna let this get in my way!' Which should have really been mine, too, but I wasn't grown up or secure enough to do that. Also I was slandered as the wanton woman in the fur rug, while Mick was the noble rock star on trial.

The 1969 festival at Altamont, the Stones' infamous free concert outside San Francisco, is now seen as a rock'n'roll Black Mass. So many things about Altamont that now seem inevitable just weren't at the time. Mick may have sung his pantomime songs about the Devil and the Midnight Rambler, but he was in a total hippie mood when he went out there to do that concert. He wanted more than anything to be part of the counterculture utopia. 'Brothers and sisters, we are creating the blueprint for a new society' and so on. That's how it was, actually. People imagine the Stones came to Altamont to incite murder, to summon up Beelzebub and his satanic crew from the bowels of the earth. Not *at all*! It was meant to be a Hippie Love Fest. It's one of the saddest things that it turned into its opposite.

Mick must have realised when 'Sympathy for the Devil' started that it was a mistake. Every time they'd play it on that tour, he'd say: 'Something funny happens when we start this.' He got off on it – as if something *might* happen if he said it. And then suddenly it wasn't funny any more. It's the same old thing: wanting to have power over people. And often they don't think about whether it's good power, whether it's positive or negative – it's part of being young and stupid.

Something happened to him out there on that tour. He'd always been so sweet and gentle – he began to get harder after that. The fact that I'd gone off to Rome with the painter Mario Schifano while he was gone didn't exactly help his mood when he returned.

All these things eroded our relationship, but there were other more fundamental problems. As much as I loved Mick, the actual life, the big rock star life, wasn't really for me. Mick, however, couldn't live any other way, and I wouldn't expect him to, it's just part of his nature.

I love Bob Dylan's attitude to the sixties. 'I am the sixties. You want 'em? You can have 'em!' Oh, God, that made me laugh so much! But, you must know by now he's a sly dog and as slippery as an eel. He's like some sort of creature that, as soon as you identify what it is, it turns into something else – a chameleon! Bob has a clever, oblique way of talking about himself. And because he's so mentally agile he can see-saw about the sixties as much as he likes. He knows you can never take him out of the sixties, however much he grumbles, so his ambivalence about *his* decade is just a prank. If you take him out of the house of cards it would collapse. He just wants to be the Joker in the pack.

Bob's old records are so embedded in our lives everybody gets nervous when a new Dylan record comes out. There's so much expectation. When *Modern Times* was released, I talked to Polly

Harvey and I told her how wonderful it was and she said, 'But, oh, I'm scared! I'm scared!' And I said, 'Don't be! It's all right! It's *more* than all right!' We always hope it's going to be this great thing – and there have been some clunkers, haven't there? Some real downers, too. *Time Out of Mind* was very negative, but, as always, there were a couple of great tracks I loved, like 'I'm Sick of Love'. I know that feeling – you want it but you get so sick of that old roller coaster.

Bob's been competing with himself since 1966, trying to outdistance his own mythology. I was listening the other day to his radio show. He was talking about fathers and there was this bit where Bob says, 'Well, you know, manic depression and depression and bipolar disorder, these are really all just the blues.' He sees everything in a mythical context. The contemporary world is ersatz, a fallen model. And then he played Lightning Hopkins. It was a wonderful moment. I thought, 'Yeah, man, that's exactly what these people are doing, taking away the lightning, taking away the blues.' The blues have that wonderful irony. I've naturally got them, I'm never going to be able to be rid of them – I couldn't bear it, I wouldn't be me.

On his show, Bob does his radio voice, the smooth, soft-talking deejay. Old possum Bob. That's what I like so much about the Dylan radio show, that he's playing a character – I love that he's gone to the trouble to create a new persona. Of course, he's always been good at manufacturing personae – brilliant. I love to see that he hasn't lost his touch. I keep thinking that I want to send him an e-mail from Marianne in Paris saying: 'Love the radio show, love the character. Don't change a thing!' But what Bob really likes to hear is young people criticising him. Because he loves saying what he really thinks. They'll say: 'Why don't you play more new music, Bob?' And he says things like: 'Well, Scott from Arlington, the thing is, there's a lot more *old* music than there is *new* music.' That's an argument I wouldn't have thought of, and so very typical of him. He basically thinks modern music is crap, but he does play it occasionally. He played a Blur track the other day called 'Coffee & TV', but most of what he plays is stuff you'll only hear on some old hipster like Hal Willner's answering machine, the wildest, oldest stuff you can imagine.

Bob still thinks of me as the angelic Marianne of the mid-sixties and whenever he sees me drinking and smoking he gets a bit cross. I'd like to say I've reformed – I have actually, I hope that doesn't disappoint – but unlike Bob I haven't found God in the process. Bob is very religious but when it gets to God and all that, I feel I have to say to him: 'You know, Bob, I'm really *not* religious actually.' I know I shouldn't say those things, but I feel I have to. I'm not a pagan or a witch or anything dark or satanic, I'm just a humanist like my dad. But it's all over the place. Religion, God, Christ on the cross. And if they're not Christians, they're Scientologists. Look at Bono, too, with his big cross and everything. I understand that people have to do what they have to do to get through, but I don't think you have to impose your thing on other people. But I do know that when you make that kind of statement to Bono, you're kind of left out, they cut you out of their plan. 'Oh, well, if she's not Christian . . .' They look askance. 'Must be something wrong there.' That's such nonsense. Christians have always done that. If you're not part of them, then you're against them, and I'm not against them, I just don't want to *be* them.

My 2002 tour promoting *Kissin' Time* ended in Australia, which is where Bob Dylan was just beginning his tour. We sat together on his balcony with a full moon shining over Sydney Harbour, talking about music – and ourselves – with a smattering of light flirtation. He told me he'd listened to my recent record, *20th Century Blues*, and that he loved Kurt Weill's chords, and he would eventually use them in those thirties-type songs on *Modern Times*. Kurt Weill took many of his melodies from music he heard in the synagogue and I'm sure Bob knew that.

I love to hear Bob talking about the blues and how we're all linked to that music. That was very good for me to hear. And folk music. How you take that music and change it by running it through your own temperament.

Bob understands my voice because he's got a funny voice too. I saw him backstage when I was about to start work on *Vagabond Ways* with Mark Howard and Daniel Lanois and he'd just worked with them. He said, 'Don't worry, it's going to be fine with them. People like us with funny voices, they've only just now figured out how to record us, and the way is *not* to use digital. You have to use analogue recording equipment.'

I love the way Bob uses his voice to create a persona. On his radio show, *Theme Time Radio Hour*, you have Ellen Barkin saying, 'It's night time, a cat howls, the high heels of a prostitute clicking down the street, the moon shows for a second and disappears behind the clouds. Here's your host, Bob Dylan.'

What amazes me about the sixties, because, in my mind, of course, it's only yesterday, is how *historic* it's become. We'll soon be lumped with the Battle of Culloden, the Peasants' Revolt, the Armada, and the invention of the loo. Over forty years ago! Longer! The strangeness of the whole passing pop parade – from Mod to Hippie to Glitter to Punk – will soon be part of the Ancientness of Olde England. It's odd, too, that the sixties, with its grand image of itself, ended not with a whimper but a bang – and woe betide any who got in the way of its thrashing apocalyptic tail.

Looking back, it wasn't such a bad idea to go to the country like Paul and Linda and not see anybody after the sixties. It was rather a wise thing to do because there was this dark cloud looming. It's like that song of Roger Waters that I sing in my show:

Do you remember me?
How we used to be
Helpless and happy and blind?
Sunk without hope
In a haze of good dope and cheap wine?
Laying on the living-room floor
On those Indian tapestry cushions you made
Thinking of calling our firstborn Jasmine or Jade.

And then that ominous chorus:

> *Don't do it*
> *Don't do it*
> *Don't do it to me!*
> *Don't think about it!*
> *Don't think about it!*
> *Don't think about what it might be*
> *Don't get up to open the door,*
> *Just stay with me here on the floor*
> *It's gonna get cold in the nineteen seventies.*

And that was written in 1968! That was prescient, if not your actual prophetic vision. Whatever we thought of Linda, and she didn't make that great an impression on me, I think it was a credit to Paul that he didn't marry a model. A module. Because that's what all the others have ended up doing, they've married these modules. And they have children who also become modules.

I heard a track from Paul McCartney's album *Ram* the other day on the radio. And with an almighty whoosh it just took me right back to those times I spent living on the streets, and then I found myself thinking about dear old Mike Leander who had been my producer on the early albums. Mike talked me into making that record that was released in 2002, called *Rich Kid Blues*. Hysterical! In fact it was never finished, and I never really liked it because it was made during my heroin addiction. This was 1972, and I was very, very sick indeed. But listening to this album now, all these years later, I think it's really rather lovely, even though my voice is very weak. What the record represents is a very important moment in my life, when I, as a junkie, was shooting up on the streets, and then suddenly this really nice man, Mike Leander, comes and finds me hanging out on some corner and makes a record with me. He somehow managed to scam some money and took me into a really cheap studio somewhere in Soho with just a guitar player. Mike played me some songs and then asked what I was listening to. I was really into Cat Stevens's haunting *Tea for the Tillerman* album, which every woman in the world seemed to love back then.

I remember that Mike played me Paul McCartney's *Ram* and I thought it was just brilliant. He said, 'Let's try and do something like this record.' And then he gave me some money to get me off the street. I actually remember leaving the studio that day with a copy of *Ram* tucked under my arm and all this cash to get some digs. That very day I managed to find a little flat and I set up home listening to Macca's wonderful record. Even now *Ram* brings a tear to my eye whenever I put it on. *Rich Kid Blues* is a sweet, folksy collection that is very redolent of the period – you know, James Taylor, Melanie and Janis Ian, that short-lived era of singer songwriters. I hoped it might fly, but then suddenly Glam Rock came along – which, as irony would have it, Mike was instrumental in because he was Gary Glitter's producer – and my poor little record was consigned for nearly thirty years to the dustbin of oblivion deep in the vaults at Gem Records. Now it seems that the record is regarded as Marianne Faithfull's 'lost album', and I guess in many ways that's right, because this album is the missing link between my early work and *Broken English*.

Sometime late in 2000 I received the proofs of a book through the post called *Turn Off Your Mind, Relax, and Float Downstream* by a member of Blondie. It's about the 'mystic sixties', and it really does capture the light and the dark side of the decade. And there *was* a lot of dark, creepy stuff in the sixties, I can tell you: The Process, Kenneth Anger, Mel Lyman, Manson, Anton LaVey, and L. Ron Hubbard. Those people were always trying to get hold of me. Somehow I managed to negotiate my way around them quite successfully. I didn't get involved in any cults, apart from going up to Bangor for that regrettable weekend with the Maharishi and the Beatles, the weekend that Brian Epstein killed himself.

It's so odd that few of my friends see *anything* negative about the sixties. Most of them from back in the day say, 'Oh but, Marianne, I don't remember the sixties like that at all . . . it was *wonderful*!' When I hear things like that I question myself, wondering if I got it all wrong and am mad. But I think I have been completely sane all along. Back in the sixties I certainly did seem to attract the most dreadful people: fringe types, cranks, weirdos, people who were after power. It was all so creepy . . .

This reminds me about the time at the tail-end of the sixties when dear Henrietta Moraes – about whom much more anon – wrote an investigative article for the *Daily Telegraph* colour supplement about L. Ron Hubbard, the founder of the Scientology religion. She infiltrated meetings in order to write her piece, which went into great detail about what she saw as the dark rotten core of what Hubbard did. She wrote all this stuff about how his partner, Mary Sue Whipp, was a homunculus with three breasts, and how he planned world domination through the power of the spirit. Hen was sure he was all about mind domination, and about muscling in on you immediately and filling your head with all this nonsense, isolating you from family and friends and brainwashing you. So of course he was furious when the *Telegraph* published Hen's article. She became convinced that people were following her around and waiting outside her house, and got so terrified that she eventually went to the police.

———————

I wanted to leave the sixties in a blaze of glory – under a volcano. That would be the Vesuvio, Spanish Tony's Million Dollar Bash, almost emblematic of the blithe, hedonistic sixties overweening-ambitions-and-*carpe-diem* approach to life. Spanish Tony was the dealer to Swinging London's stars and the *jeunesse dorée*.

All of London's rock aristocracy were in attendance the evening Spanish Tony, nefarious drug dealer to the stars, finally opened his nightclub (which had, actually, only one night). Like all dealers, he didn't consider himself just a dealer, he wanted to be something else, something a bit more grand, a maître d' to the hipoisie. Thus, the Vesuvio.

It was pretty much of a dive, but the people there were just stupendous: *le tout Londres hip*. All the Beatles, most of the Stones, a few Whos, spangled guitar slingers, mangled drummers were there – in short, everybody who was anybody, or thought they were. The punch had, of course, been spiked with LSD. And in strolls Paul – very casually, very cool, almost whistling, you know, with one of those little smiles on his lips as if he's got a really big secret. John was already there and seemed to have had quite a bit of punch by the time we arrived. George, too, of course, and Pattie Boyd, the quintessence of Pop chic. So there's our Paulie, looking rather pleased with himself. He was in fact very cool, a real man-about-town and interested in different things than George. Curious Paul, fascinated with all sorts of strange things – he really was like that. And what swinging scene would be complete without Robert Fraser, Groovy Bob – the title of Harriet Vyner's biography, a bricolage portrait of the archetypal boulevardier of swinging London. The Robert Fraser Gallery was the place to be. He showed the classic Pop artists of the sixties – Richard Hamilton, Jim Dine, and Andy Warhol – and made avant-garde art hip to the rock princelings. He was beautiful, took a lot of drugs, and could always be found where the new thing was happening. 'More than any other figure I can think of, Robert Fraser personifies the Sixties as I remember them,' so blurbed Lord McCartney on the back of the Vyner bio. Robert even tried to turn Paul on to heroin, but Paul didn't care for the experience – that was lucky!

So there we were, all having a wonderful time, really high and even a little bit of alcohol, which to us was anathema. It was punch, which is easy to drink and a rather delicious sort of drunk. Little did we know what was in it. Finally we decide to drink, and it was acid! And then in the middle of all this, Paul, sidling about with his hands behind his back.

'What have you got behind your back, Paul?' we are crying out.

'Oh, nothing, really,' says he. 'Just something, um, we've just done.' *Knowing* that everyone would say, 'Oh! Play it!'

Well, the thing about the Vesuvio that was really great was the speakers. That's where all of our money had gone, on the very best speakers, *huge* speakers, the biggest that you could possibly get. Everything else was on the floor, of course; just *loads* of cushions. Come to think of it, the set-up would never have worked as a club, but Tony wasn't one to get hung up on the details. For a private party, however, it was perfect. So there was a lot of 'Oh, go on, Paul, please!' You know, you always had to do that with him, basically.

'Oh, yeah, all right, then,' he says. And then he proceeds to put on 'Hey, Jude'. It just went – *boom*! – straight to the chest. It was the first time anyone had ever heard it, and we were all just *blown away*. And then, of course, we couldn't stop playing it, we just played away, mixed up with a bit of Little Richard and some blues.

What a night! Right then you just knew how lucky you were to live in these times, with this crowd. That song was so impossible to describe or even take in that I didn't know what to *say* to Paul, but of course I did go up to him (we were a polite little lot) and probably burbled, 'Wow! Far *out*, man!' The required string of incoherent sounds, but I felt I had to say something even though, the state I was in, I could hardly speak. Even Mick said it was fantastic, because it *was*. I guess most people would think the Stones may have had mixed feelings at that moment, and perhaps they did. But (possibly due to the laced punch) the main feeling was one of: aren't *we* all the greatest bunch of young geniuses to grace the planet and isn't this the most amazing time to be alive. It was as if only with this group and at *that* moment could Paul have done it. We had a sense of everybody being in the right place, at the right time, with the right people. And every time something came out, like 'I Can See for Miles and Miles' or 'Jumpin' Jack Flash', 'Visions of Johanna', or the sublime 'God Only Knows' from *Pet Sounds,* or anything at all, it seemed like we had just broken another sound barrier. Blind Faith, the Mothers of Invention . . . one amazing group after another. Tiny Tim, *anything*, we were instant fans! And I don't *think* it was just the drugs.

It was one of the most incestuous music scenes ever. And how did they all *find* each other? And how did they all seem to be in the perfect group *for them*? Most knew that they were, but some, like Eric Clapton, kept jumping about trying to find exactly his right space and never quite finding it. But even that made sense for him. If not for the peregrine wanderings of Eric we would never have had 'Layla' and all that. Experimental Eric, mixing it up with different bands: Derek and the Dominos, Greg Allman, Delaney & Bonnie, Blind Faith. He was in so many different bands – a restless troubadour. In the end, though, all this wandering about from group to group made him into a separate entity: Eric Clapton. He's his own brand.

The Vesuvio may have limped along for another couple of weeks before it closed. Of course, the whole venture was a very dangerous idea; it would have been a place where people went to score. Definitely needed, of course, but somewhat unwise. How tempting it must have been to all – a sort of one-stop shop: you go to the club and you get the drugs right there. It would have made life easier for Spanish Tony because instead of having to drive down to John and Yoko and then to me and then drive to Robert, he could just lie on his cushions and make money. Convenient, yes, but also quite convenient for the local constabulary!

I think Spanish Tony's fear of immediate arrest may have been unfounded. Probably the first thing that would have happened would have been the local fuzz saying, 'Okay, how much are you going to pay us?'

In my mind's eye the last image of that night is this: John and Yoko, both completely legless, deciding to drive themselves in the psychedelic Rolls over to Ringo's old flat on Montagu Square. They would've crashed and killed themselves. Driving wasn't John's forte, never mind the acid. I see Spanish Tony, keeping himself cool on coke and smack, rushing out and putting them in a taxi. He hands the driver a twenty-quid note and tells him, 'Don't let them out till you get to 38 Montagu Square.'

There's a picture in my mind's eye of Mick and Keith in front of the Vesuvio with its painting of Mount Vesuvius behind them. So very camp. Mount Vesuvius was an apropos image for swinging London. We were all living underneath a volcano, getting high, getting dressed, getting together, swanning about in clubs with witty names while forces we hadn't even guessed existed were about to fall down on us. Scintillating, vibrating creatures in fantastically beautiful clothes from Ossie Clark and the Antique Market, all frolicking beneath a volcano on the verge of erupting.

i guess she kept those vagabond ways

Singing Kurt Weill and Bertolt Brecht for two years was
incredibly good for my writing. The bar shot right up. Not that
I can now write like Bertolt Brecht or Kurt Weill, but still the
experience of singing their songs on my sabbatical, as I call it,
changed my way of thinking about songs – and the point of
view of the song's narrator. A kind of charged ambivalence that
inflects all the imagery.

Vagabond Ways is quite a dark record – which is my speciality
as I do dark quite well! I had to go into that gothic space and
I didn't have to take heroin to do it. It's the most unrepentant
of my recent albums, but then, I hadn't done anything so bad
recently that I had to repent for except . . . well, let's not go into
that right now.

By the time I came to record *Vagabond Ways* in 1999 I had
been well marinated in the Brecht/Weill canon. It was like
going back to school. You really learn how to use a song to tell
a story.

The song, 'Vagabond Ways', was written with Dave Courts, my dear old friend and hip jeweller – Keith's skull rings. I came across a little piece in the *New York Herald Tribune*, where I do get a lot of material. The article talked about how in Sweden they hadn't stopped their sterilisation initiative until 1974. These were programmes used to sterilise drug addicts, homeless people, nymphomaniacs and alcoholics. I was surprised.

And when I read about this hideous practice I thought, 'Oh, here's a song!' So I put myself into the character of the girl about to be sterilised. She's talking to the doctor. And then at the very end it just says, 'It was a long time ago.' They took her child away. And she was sterilised. She died of the drink and the drugs, but yes I guess she kept those vagabond ways . . .

It's quite subtle, you know. Nobody ever believed me when I told them there is an actual story there. And a subject – other than myself. It's quite hopeless. Everybody always thinks everything I write is about me.

Of course there are some parallels or I wouldn't be interested in the story in the first place. I've got to feel some empathy with this girl. But at the same time when I write a song or perform any of the songs, they're *stories*. 'Broken English' was about Ulrika Meinhof. It wasn't till years later that I understood that it could be about me, too.

'Incarceration of a Flower Child' is a Roger Waters song. But how perfect a lyric is that! It had so many reverberations about the sixties, the end of the sixties and the consequences. It's possibly about Syd Barrett, the founder and original lead singer of Pink Floyd, who became deranged as a result of obsessive drug-taking in 1967 and spent most of his life in institutions – a legendary loon. He died in July 2006. But songs are composites, they're about many different things, not just the ostensible subject. Roger wrote 'Incarceration of a Flower Child' in 1968 but he never gave it to Pink Floyd.

Speaking of the past, 'File it Under Fun' is my way of dealing with my history. It's about anybody I'd ever really loved. The title may sound a bit flip, but it's not intended to be *that* ironic; it's more true to my life, true to my feelings than sardonic. It's got a kind of it's-all-right-now feel, we'll file it under fun, don't worry about it. It's true there's a certain world weariness to it, but that's probably because I'm always being asked about my past and it does get wearying. That was my reply at the time I wrote it anyway. I may have changed; *Vagabond Ways* is a long time ago.

The title, 'Wilder Shores of Love', is taken from Lesley Blanch's book of the same name, about the exotic and possessed lives of four wild women who lived as they wished: Isabelle Eberhardt, Aimee Dubucq de Rivery, Jane Digby and Isabel Burton. But wilder shores of love has a bit more personal reference than just the book. It came from a line of Anita's. She said she'd been to the wilder shores of love. Not sure I have! Love to me is much more practical. Maybe she had just had some great sex. I have, too, but I wouldn't exactly describe it as the wilder shores of love.

'For Wanting You' comes from my asking Elton and Bernie Taupin to write a song for me – and that's what they came up with. It was a wonderful moment when I received that in the post. Of course, as per usual, I did not do it in the most commercial way you can imagine. I'm sure it could've been a hit, a big hit, but I underplayed it.

'Great Expectations', written with Daniel Lanois, is the story of my life. It's the story in my mind as it goes through my life in pictures. It's as if you're sitting outside a tent around a fire and I'm telling the story. As I recount it I can't remember everything that's happened and, truth being so subjective, it's a fable rather than an autobiography. The exclusiveness of memory as it fuses with the mythical life story and with Dickens's wistful novel. It's a slightly bitter little song.

To do a song like 'Tower of Song' with a light touch is quite hard. The tendency is to be earnest and intense, so it isn't easy to pull off. But I think I'm getting over that. Still, you have to approach 'Tower of Song' like the great monument it is, a Tower of Babel of all songs and all the great singers who've gone before you, including the haunting voice of Leonard Cohen himself. The way Leonard does it is dark and broody. I lightened it up a bit. Some people didn't like that, but there's no way you can out-gothicise Leonard Cohen.

'After the Ceasefire' is a Frank McGuinness bit of magic. It's a very Irish song, and quite literal in that sense. It's not about Ireland, it's about a relationship, but also Frank's relationship *with* Ireland. Just a lovely lovely lovely little poem.

It was all the others' fault, they thought at any rate
After the ceasefire to put an end to hate
She was reaching for her knife, he a fork and spoon
They sat about devouring the poison of the moon
Shared a fatal cigarette neither one would light
Their breath was flame enough, nobody said goodnight
After the ceasefire, after the ceasefire.

FRANK McGUINNESS and DANIEL LANOIS,
'After the Ceasefire'

Vagabond Ways I recorded with Dan, and Mark Howard, in the Teatro, the recording studio that belongs to Daniel Lanois. Mark produced it. Dan and I wrote some songs together – beautiful stuff. I'm not particularly fond of what he does with U2, but his own records I love. And the ones he does with Emmylou Harris and Bob Dylan, of course – *Oh Mercy* and *Time Out of Mind*. That wonderful song 'She's gone with the man with the long black coat . . .'

What was going on in my life when I was making this record? I was emerging from my cocoon. I'm very one-pointed. I'd done *20th Century Blues* and then *The Seven Deadly Sins*. So *Vagabond Ways* was my first record back in my own genre. I felt I had to make a bit of a statement. A Mariannifesto. To say, 'Here I am! I'm back!'

looking back at anger

In early 1970 I was in bad shape. Not long after I'd left Mick I
found myself on a slippery slope – I'd become a heroin addict
and spent my days seeking oblivion, sitting on the wall of a
demolished building in Soho. As if things weren't dire enough,
I agreed to play Lilith, a cemetery-haunting female demon, in
Kenneth Anger's occult allegory *Lucifer Rising*. Needless to say,
the film didn't improve my situation, either karmically or
financially. And that was that – or so I thought, but karma has
an awkward habit of bouncing back at you. It reminded me, yet
again, that dabbling in the occult – even if you don't entirely
believe in its coiled powers – has a nasty way of casting its
baleful influence long after you have left the scene – and
accumulating vengeful force along the way.

Through William Burroughs I'd met the writer and painter
Brion Gysin – inventor of the cut-up and Burroughs's sometime
collaborator. Brion was a really kind soul. When I was living on
the street in London, I would occasionally go and see him. He
was one of those rare people who genuinely did care about you;
he was different, especially in those dark troubled times in

London, Brion stood out like a beacon when everyone else seemed so self-centred and horrible – there was little sympathy for someone in my state in those days.

One day Brion took me round to where the occult filmmaker Kenneth Anger, whom I'd met through Robert Fraser, was staying. Kenneth was notorious for his film *Scorpio Rising*, a montage of Hell's Angels, Hitler, fellatio, sodomy, Jesus, and assorted satanic imagery. Anger has made some two dozen movies, almost all dealing with satanic subject matter; aside from *Scorpio Rising*, the best known are *Invocation of My Demon Brother*, and *Inauguration of the Pleasure Dome*. I should have run as fast as I could from a self-styled conjurer of dark powers – however silly his dilettantish Satanism seemed to me – but I was very susceptible to the influence of others just then and easily led. As my father would have reminded me, in the words of Virgil, *facilis descensus Averno* – easy is the descent to Hell.

But love and light to Kenneth – only thing to do with Kenneth – love and light I send. Really. Can't do anything else. I've gone through so much recently. All the anger, bitterness, upsetness, paranoia, grief has gone away. Hopefully, for good.

At the time I met him, Kenneth was living in Robert Fraser's flat – Robert was in India. Kenneth saw that I was very vulnerable, obviously anorexic, on drugs, nowhere to live, and wanted to help me by putting me in his film. He didn't understand my reasons for being on the wall, but saw that I could definitely be *used*, and that, in a nutshell, was how I came to be in *Lucifer Rising*.

Kenneth really believed that he was setting me on my feet again as an actress. He thought I was on his side, which in a sense I was – as an artist. But basically he didn't have a clue what I was up to – or how fragile I was. On junk, at the end of my tether and in no shape to do anything – let alone play a graveyard-haunting Mesopotamian night demon with a penchant for destroying children. Actually, since the advent of 'cosmic feminism', Lilith has become something of a heroine of women's rights. In the Talmud she was the first wife of Adam, but refused to accept her subservient role. Adam rejected her, after which God created Eve as a more obedient mate. Because she refused to accept the inferior relationship in the primal marriage, she has been interpreted as a strong-minded woman reacting to male oppression. In Hebrew folklore she is said to have slept with Lucifer, giving birth to hundreds of lilin, female demons who would become the succubi of medieval and Jewish legend.

Whew! Kenneth got me at a very weak moment – I was completely dependent on the kindness of strangers, and, in fact, met a lot of *very kind* strangers. My friends the meths drinkers, for example, and the people in the Chinese laundry and my drug dealer – well! – and all sorts of funny, generous people I ran into. Even the police looked after me.

Strangely, Kenneth thought he could take me, a heroin addict, off the street, transport me to Egypt, and get me to play Lilith. It was great to go to Egypt – don't get me wrong – but to have to crawl around an Arab graveyard dressed as a nun covered in Max Factor blood with skulls all around me was *insane*! It's amazing they didn't stone me to death, actually. The scene was shot very early in the morning when nobody was around, thank God. Of course today I'd probably be on some list of infidel dogs for desecrating a Muslim graveyard in *a movie*. Anyway, lightning didn't strike – but, of course, it did eventually.

Naturally it was a *huge* mistake. Karmically a *seriously* wrong turn for me and something that took me a long time to overcome. I never should have done it, and had I been in my right mind I wouldn't have considered it for a minute. That was one of the problems of being as high as I was at that moment, that somebody like Kenneth Anger – who is definitely on the dark side – could come along and get me to do mad, satanic things. What did I think I was doing? Well, I thought it was art, I suppose. I never got paid, which I always think is a sure sign it's art. It *was* art, wasn't it? It was the Devil's art, and it's very hard to get paid by the Devil, as you may know. There's a few other people we could put in that category – mainly from the music business.

But before I get any further into the less charming aspects of Kenneth's character I want to bang on a bit about the good things he did, because so far I've only given you his ruthless side.

One memorable evening Kenneth took me to see Christopher Marlowe's *Tamburlaine* at the National Theatre. Kenneth was naturally a huge fan of Marlowe, that Elizabethan 'student of the School of Night' whose death – a blow to the head by his own knife – is often seen as being foretold in his bloody and

demon-haunted plays. 'Black is the beauty of the brightest day,'
he has the ruthless tyrant Tamburlaine boast. *Tamburlaine* –
parts I and II – is awe-inspiring and grotesque in an epic sort of
way that only Elizabethans and Jacobeans could manage. I am
grateful to Kenneth for that, even though it was three or four
hours of disembowellings and upside-down crucifixions and tits
being cut off and children being slashed. 'Blood is the god of
war's rich livery.' Endless horrors, but still *fantastic*. Kenneth
was *drooling* throughout, and so was I, Christopher Marlowe
being one of my heroes, too. Marlowe had his profligate vision,
his wayward, possessed intent and conception of himself as the
doomed, 'brain-sick' artist ('What is beauty, saith my sufferings,
then?'). I'm always impressed when I see monstrous happenings
turn into art before my eyes. When you see *Tamburlaine*, or any
Christopher Marlowe play, you are confronted with *actual*
genius, with a metamorphosis of horror into art. The great
Elizabethan 'blank-verse beast' whirls words like a conjurer
juggling sapphires, swords, stars, and the axle-tree of heaven as
if they were so many balls:

> *I hold the Fates bound fast in iron chains,*
> *And with my hand turn Fortune's wheel about;*
> *And sooner shall the sun fall from his sphere*
> *Than Tamburlaine be slain or overcome.*

Heavens! You truly believe some word-mad god tunes this
music to our souls.

On the other hand, I'm afraid I've never really felt that *Lucifer
Rising* was art. To be kind, let's say the jury is still out on it.

The thing is, for me it's just sort of undigested cult stuff. There's no question that it fits exquisitely well into this ghastly world we live in, but there's a difference. I didn't have a very high opinion of him to begin with and after I'd seen the alchemical films of Harry Smith I realised where Kenneth must've got many of his images from. The idea of drawing flying saucers coming into the screen – that was Harry's idea. You could say Kenneth nicked it or you could say he was influenced by Harry, depending on how generous we want to be. Or we could say they influenced each other – which may well be the case. Harry started out as a fan of Kenneth's work.

Harry, in any case, was at the other end of the spectrum. He was cool and relaxed – he didn't have to promote himself. Kenneth tries too hard. Harry wouldn't have minded whatever I said about him. He could take a joke, but Ken can't – which is something I learned when I wrote my last book.

I suppose I was a bit unfair to Kenneth in my autobiography. The way I described my experiences was honest – the whole fiasco was so disturbing I still flinch when I think about it – but at the same time, I understand why Kenneth was so upset.

Obviously he was expecting a delightful, charming portrait of himself instead of what he got. I suppose I was pretty harsh, even a wee bit nasty, and now I'm trying to see it from his point of view – which isn't all that easy. But, whatever I said about him, I certainly didn't expect the vituperative response I got. Sometime after the book came out, Kenneth sent me a letter containing a curse written in fake blood.

I opened it up and basically flipped out. I was so troubled by it I immediately took it down to my friends, Julian and Victoria Lloyd, to figure out what to do. On one level the letter was silly and hysterically funny, too. There was the part where he says, 'You Jew! You Jew, like Kirk Douglas, like DANNY KAYE!' What kind of curse is that? A Hollywood witch's curse, I imagine, right out of Vampira's *grimoire*. It was all about Jews and Danny Kaye – because Danny Kaye was Jewish, not a fact you would be likely to focus on, but Kenneth, of course, would (being virulently anti-Semitic). I've got a lovely Jewish granny, thank God, from whom I got my blonde hair and the big lips. Kenneth knew about all that. This put a rabid bee in his bonnet.

He's been going on about my being part Jewish for years. He's given *lectures* about it, about 'my flaw'. I've heard from other people about this terrible flaw in my character: the fact that I am Jewish! That was funny and silly; I just laughed at that. But then the really vile stuff started to spew out: 'DIE OF LUNG CANCER!' and all that generic malice right out of the *Common Book of Beastly Spells*. For someone who considers himself a magus scrying out his victim's secrets, he somehow missed a few critical things that might have hit home to me rather more effectively. Like sleeping pills! You'll die from an overdose of sleeping pills! Or painkillers. He missed all that. Kenneth was quite capable of picking out the one thing that would truly sting you. The curse he sent to poor Robert Fraser had nothing in it except a razor blade and a piece of type saying: 'Something to cure your stutter.'

I joke about it, but at the time I was *absolutely* panicked, holding the vile curse in my hands – not a fun thing to have in one's possession. I went down to Jules and Vic's – they were still living on the corner by Leixlip Castle then and showed it to them. Victoria was appalled but Julian was giddily impressed. 'It's a masterpiece!' he declared. 'You've got to send it to the V&A!' I don't know exactly what the Victoria & Albert Museum would've made of it, but *visually* it was an astonishing item. Very graphic and ghastly at the same time, and as maliciously conceived as only a true Satanist and twisted individual could conjure up. It was this *huge* piece of paper with threats inscribed in blood – Max Factor blood, I'm sure, completely fake – but as an artefact it *looked* incredible. It was a big, malign, poisonous curse – maybe a bit too wordy, maybe he raged on a bit too much. I mean, does the Devil *rant* you to death?

'What the hell!' I *screamed* at Julian. 'I know it's sort of wonderful in a ghastly cult artefact sort of way. It would be fine if it went to someone else, but it came to me, and, um, I can't exactly look at it as an aesthetic object just now.'

In the end, Victoria told me to take it to the crossroads where there was a Lady Chapel and burn it with salt, rosemary and rue. Where would I find rue in this day and age? In Vic's garden. Victoria is not a witch and does not grow this stuff for magical purposes. It's just a herb, a lovely, old-fashioned herb. It's in the wonderful mad scene in *Hamlet:* 'rue for remembrance'. Or was it rosemary?

OPHELIA: *There's rosemary, that's for remembrance. Pray you, love, remember. And there is pansies, that's for thoughts.*

LAERTES: *A document in madness!*

But, why burn Kenneth's hideous screed with rosemary when it was something I clearly *didn't* want to remember? I did it in order to remember my true self. And mark that this nonsense from Kenneth had got nothing to do with me. To fight back. For him to remember who he's dealing with and for me to know who I am.

Kenneth must have been terribly roiled by what I said about him in my book, but I didn't mean to hurt him. I just said what I really thought, like I do, but one has to have compassion. I realise now, in hindsight, that Kenneth was half using me, and half trying to help me, and in a funny way, I accept that and I can say 'thank you', but at the same time, it caused me a hell of a lot of trouble. I should have just said 'no'. I don't mean I was ready to reform completely, but I should have said no. 'No thank you, darling, perhaps we'll practise one of your satanic rituals some other time!' If you let somebody do things to you, such as using you as an actress in a demonic ritual, you will pay a price. Let's face it, it's dabbling in darkness and it's no joke. It's down to a question of darkness and light, and I'm not even talking about it in religious terms because I'm not a religious person. I have my own spiritual track, but I'm certainly not religious. In fact, I'm *against* religion, and that helped me, of course, to avoid being drawn into Kenneth's sway, because black magic *is* a religion.

I, of course, did not tell Kenneth what I'd done – burning his letter at a wayside shrine – because in some Harry Potterish way he could have made a counter curse to that, too. It's quite complicated, this whole business. And you have to be very careful. What I didn't want to do – which in fact you *can* do – was to send the curse back to Kenneth so that it would land on him. Within the occult scheme of things if you send out that much hatred against someone and the recipient has enough power to hurl it back at you psychically, it can rebound – like the piece of paper with the spell on it that Dana Andrews slips back into the magician's pocket at the end of *Curse of the Demon*. I'm not an expert, needless to say, but it's a wearying and aggravating business.

I do think my counter-attack worked. I somehow knew intuitively what to do. In that way I'm quite like my mother – I've got that side to me, I just choose not to go to the dark side. White magic is another story entirely – that I am quite capable of using – and this is what you must do if you're ever unfortunate enough to get a poison-pen letter from Kenneth.

Perhaps by playing a demoness I had summoned up long-dormant demons, some ghoulish skull-fondling jinni out of the desert wastes – but what is quite certain is that demons will fasten on you when you are at your weakest point and by toying with them, even in a film, you give them power. As Christopher Marlowe says at the conclusion of *Doctor Faustus*, his hero's fate for meddling in dark matters should make wise men pause before dabbling in 'unlawful things'

Whose deepness doth entice such forward wits
To practice more than heavenly power permits.

And I didn't *entirely* rely on my magical practices. In a very
English way I wrote him a stiff letter in which I said, 'Now,
look, Kenneth, I've supported you, I've always said how great
you are, and you know what a big fan of your films I am . . .'
blah-di-blah-blah – I mentioned everything I'd ever done or
said about him – 'so *do not* go into a queenie fit about the book.
Please let's have no more of this nonsense!'

He wrote back – a much calmer Kenneth. But then at the end
of his letter he added: 'Unfortunately, I *can't* take the curse
back.'

eva

My mother had been another person entirely before the war. I always had a hard time imagining what she was like as a cool, urbane, young Weimar girl. It certainly didn't carry over into her life with us. The war must have changed her drastically. She was only twenty-four when the *Anschluss* happened and overnight a precious part of her life was simply ripped away.

As my mother got older, she talked more and more about her parents. It was always a very idealistic portrait, with no unpleasant scenes whatever. Her childhood had been perfect.

Even though I never saw much of this Weimar side to Eva, I must have imbibed it somehow in my mother's milk – it's the only explanation I have for how I was able to do the Kurt Weill material so believably. Doing these songs takes an aptitude for seeing the grotesque as an aspect of love. Kurt Weill/Bertolt Brecht songs are the counterpoint to the unsettling paintings of Otto Dix and George Grosz. The style was called the *Neue Sachlichkeit*, New Realism, but actually it's a celebration of the edge between beauty and the bizarre. That's really what the

Brecht/Weill canon is all about. You've got to be able to go there. That wonderfully masochistic chorus in 'Surabaya Johnny', for example. The sheer erotic perversity of it.

> *Surabaya Johnny. Will the hurt ever mend?*
> *Surabaya Johnny. Oh, I burn at your touch.*
> *You got no heart, Johnny, but oh, I love you,*
> *I love you, I love you so much.*

They're all like that. You can hear it in Pirate Jenny's song, her all-consuming quest for vengeance in *The Threepenny Opera* — something my mother understood all too well: the ship, the ominous black ship, sailing into the harbour.

As a person Eva was much warmer than my father and I'm more like her in that respect. But of course that emotional side of her had a downside. She could erupt in an irrational fury. My father's detachment was oddly soothing compared to my mother's rages. He didn't get so emotionally involved, and his remoteness, which I often lamented, was reassuring amidst the family turmoil.

My mother was extreme in her passions: her likes, her dislikes, her resentments. She was an almost *savage* person. Sophisticated and refined on a certain level, but utterly dominated by hatred and love and regret and bitterness. She first became embittered about my father, later on it was me. But long before either of us had failed her, she was a tinderbox. Drinking made it worse.

Unlike my father, my mother wasn't intellectual. And as she got older and her past began to weigh on her, she became very religious. She suffered from melancholia – that was her word for it. Something like depression, but a much more romantic concept: a gloomy state of mind saturated in Middle-European *Weltschmerz*, the sense that one's own sorrow is intrinsically linked to the sadness of the world.

I remember going to church with my mother when I was young and watching her getting incredibly emotional – praying loudly with tears streaming down her face, racked with sobs actually. I was terribly embarrassed. Of course she had just been through the war, but children don't really understand that. When it finally dawned on me that her involvement with the church brought her peace, I felt glad for her – and then very magnanimously forgave her for embarrassing me.

At the end of her life, God and Christ, Heaven and Hell, all those emblematic ideas became terrifyingly real to her. I suppose she was concerned about going to Hell. She had shot a man, after all. When the Russians entered Vienna at the end of the war, they were hellbent on rape, destruction, and pillage. They opened all the wine cellars in Vienna. Wine running down the streets; all the Russian soldiers had to do was open their mouths and the wine ran in. They got blind drunk, and then raped every woman in sight. A Russian soldier from the steppes burst into the room where my mother and grandmother were hiding. He raped my mother and was about to rape my grandmother, at which point Eva picked up a gun and shot him. It was justifiable homicide, of course – but murder in the eyes of the church.

As a result of the rape my mother had to have an abortion. After the Russians came to Vienna, there were long lines of women queuing up to have abortions. I've heard that when a woman has had an abortion, she always wants to have a child. Certainly, this explains why Eva wanted to marry my father and have me.

After my parents divorced, my mother and I moved into 41 Milman Road in Reading. I was about seven at the time and, looking back, I can see that Eva was relatively happy when in Reading. She was teaching and I was going to school and things were okay, but I don't think she realised it until long after it was over. I've found that the ability to realise you're happy while it's happening is actually quite elusive.

Eva got a job teaching maladjusted children, as they were then called: children from broken homes who'd gone through hellish lives. And of course she was very good at it. Filled with empathy, she taught them dance, current affairs and art. Eva taught a type of free dance, very much like Isadora Duncan. The children danced in bare feet, made symbolic gestures, and acted out expressive scenes. Sometimes I would go to her classes, which was quite a strange experience. These kids were very disturbed; they had gone through truly terrible experiences and some had done horrible things. I remember one boy had killed some kittens, and he was obviously going to grow up to be a psychopath. That was my unforgiving, childlike take on it.

If I saw them being rude to my mother, I would freak out and yell at them, which did no good whatsoever. Eva, in a very matter-of-fact way, would just give them a smack – not hard, but just a quick clip, like a mother lion.

Eva also taught dance at my school for a while and I found myself put into one of her productions. At fourteen, I was playing the lead in *The Snow Queen* and, right in the middle of the performance, I got my first period. There was blood on my white costume, and even worse I had absolutely no idea what it was. My mother took no notice.

'The show must go on,' she said. 'Just ignore it.'

———————

When he was a young man my mother's father fell in love and married an eighteen-year-old Jewish girl from Hungary. Coming from his aristocratic family this was a highly unusual thing to do – and of course his family opposed the marriage, but her family even more violently. One time Eva's grandmother asked her to go to the synagogue with her, and Eva refused. She had been brought up a Catholic and Catholics aren't supposed to attend other people's churches. Many years later Eva still regretted it, which was probably why she became so ecumenical when she got older.

When the Nazis came to power in Vienna they insisted Jews wear the Star of David on their arms. My grandfather was outraged that his wife should be subjected to this indignity and said to my mother: 'Come on, Eva, we're going to visit the head of the Gestapo, and we'll see about this!' He put on his Tyrolean hat and his cloak – he was very tall and imposing – and as he strode along the street in a *fury,* my mother, quite frightened by the whole business, was trying to keep up with him. Eventually they got to the Gestapo headquarters and my grandfather announced himself.

'Baron Sacher-Masoch,' he said. 'I demand to see the officer in charge!' They were shown in to the office of the head of the Gestapo in Vienna, who turned out to be an ensign in my grandfather's regiment in the First World War.

'What's this nonsense about my wife having to wear a Star of David?' my grandfather asked him. 'I want you to cancel that order *immediately*.' And this officer – my mother always used to call him by some daft German name like *Bumpfelkaeger* – who clearly hero-worshipped my grandfather, answered immediately: 'Oh, *mein Kolonel*, *mein Kolonel*, it is fine, it is fine, sir. I'll give you the papers right now. Of course, Frau Baroness Sacher-Masoch doesn't have to wear the Star of David.'

And with that he gave my grandfather the documents exempting her. My grandfather snatched up the papers and swept out of the room. As he got to the doorway, he stopped and turned back and fixed Herr Bumpfelkaeger in his sights, head of Gestapo in Austria, a very powerful man, and said: 'If I had known in the First World War what you were going to become, I would have shot you in the trenches!'

Despite the fact that my grandmother had converted to
Christianity, she still attended synagogue on high holy days.
Conversion was not uncommon among Jews in Austria at that
time. For instance, Karl Kraus, the famous aphorist, gadfly, and
playwright, was an assimilated Jew. That's why the Second
World War and the Nazi racial laws came as such a shock.
Many people felt that first and foremost they were Germans or
Austrians or Hungarians. My grandmother thought of herself as
a Hungarian patriot. She'd grown up in Hungary and had
strong feelings about Hungarian independence even though she
was married to an Austrian army officer.

As I grew older I got a far more edgy picture of my mother's
past than the one I had previously heard from her. One curious
story about my mother's past life in the Weimar Republic takes
place on the Kurfürstendamm, the equivalent of Fifth Avenue
in Berlin, where all the fancy shops – and prostitutes – were.

One night my mother was coming back from dancing and
befriended a streetwalker. In the Weimar period, streetwalkers
used to put little red reflector lights in their high heels; that's
how you could tell they were whores. When Eva crossed the
Kurfürstendamm to go to her apartment, which was in a rough
area, this girl would walk with her and protect her. They would
talk along the way about this and that and how much they had
in common despite the differences in their lives. That, at least,
was my mother's story. In her telling, this pretty prostitute drops
my mother off at her house and there the story ends. I've
always wondered what happened next, but I was too young and
afraid to ask. My mother was somewhat bisexual, but this didn't

help her understand my own proclivity in this area. Eva had been quite wild and bohemian when she was young, but by the time I knew her, she had changed into another person entirely. Motherhood does that. But she still had the odd girlfriend – and certainly boyfriends. I can see that one of the reasons I was sent to the convent was so that my mother could have a sex life.

In my mother's past I sensed strange currents beneath the surface. There are pictures, for instance, of my mother dressed up in boys' clothes, snapshots of her in tights and doublets as if she were doing a Shakespeare play – it was an interesting, free time and I'm pretty sure Eva was in the thick of it. She had friends who were costume designers and set designers and painters and dancers and prostitutes and writers, and one or two very rich boyfriends, as well. She was living the high life until the *Anschluss* happened.

After the Nazis came in of course everything changed. She could easily have left. She had done her first Hollywood film test in the early thirties and they wanted her out there. I could never understand why she didn't just go. She said it was because she couldn't leave her people, and there always was something really rather noble about my mother in a crisis. She came of age in a time of perpetual crisis – afterwards, normal life was a little more difficult for her. My father admired my mother's courage. Theirs was a classic wartime romance. Afterwards, they must have found out just how incredibly different they were. The romance of the war, the danger they found themselves in – Glynn was a spy and Eva his connection – was very romantic. And Eva was so beautiful – but of course very, very spoilt, and Glynn was not the sort of person who was going to indulge her whims.

When I was young my mother still had extravagant habits. Even in little things there was a huge difference between Eva's and Glynn's attitudes. As a child I used to spread oodles of butter on my toast – heart-attack amounts. I'd lather it on so thickly that you could barely see the toast. My father would go absolutely nuts.

'What on earth do you think you're doing?' he would growl, eyeing the ton of butter on my toast. And this would cause rows between my parents, with my mother saying, 'She can put on any amount she wants to.' And this would go on and on. I guess it was just before the end of post-war rationing that in Britain went on right into the mid-fifties.

The war had taught my father to be frugal, but it had taught my mother something altogether different. The war years in Vienna had been very hard for her – there was no margarine, let alone butter – so she decided that now was the time to have as much butter as possible, not to mention anything else that had been rationed. As a child I would have *mounds* of cherries and apples and bananas. I loved Eva's domestic recklessness, but as she got older my mother became more like my father, a change in attitude that I could hardly believe. In her mind she went back to the austerity of the war years; I think a lot of this had to do with her friends, who were far more effective at curbing her extravagances than my father ever was.

My mother ended up very like Henrietta's – the 'mustn't grumble' approach to life that came out of the war years. I remember as she got older, when she would run a bath, she would only fill it up four inches, and I would say: 'Why are you doing that? Why don't you pour yourself a really good bath, because your back's bad and it would be so good for you.'

'Oh, no, no, no, during the war, you know, we . . .' she would say. I don't know if they could even take baths in Vienna during the war. She turned into the type of thrifty, cautious *Hausfrau* Austrian she had never been. Like the Germans, Austrians as a people are very frugal. Frugality or *Sparsamkeit*, 'thriftiness', is seen as a virtue and very highly prized in those countries and extends to everything: food, water, clothes. In Eva's case, I felt she was playing the martyr, and it didn't work on me.

The other thing I managed to find out from Eva was that my grandmother had desperately wanted to be a doctor, but of course at the time that was completely out of the question. This beautiful, young Jewish girl wanting to go to Paris to study medicine and there was no way this could ever have happened. One of the messages that came through very clearly from my mother was that women should do what they want, follow their dreams and follow their heart and not just get married and be adornments to their husbands.

But, unlike my father, Eva wasn't proud of my success. She couldn't really understand my pop stuff and by the time I started to do the Kurt Weill and Bertolt Brecht material she was dead. She would have loved it. I don't think she appreciated *Broken English* any more than my father. She didn't get it at all. She was very Edwardian in that way, and what I was doing didn't translate into anything she could understand. If I'd made a lot of money from my singing and been able to keep her in the style to which she yearned to become accustomed, everything would have been fine, but I was never able to do that. Money has always been a problem for me – it's a problem now and it was a problem then. But I make a good living from my work and I'm very grateful for that.

Speaking of which, my mother really liked Mick. Mick was wonderful; I was the bad one. Why that was, I don't know, but that's how she saw it. And of course Mick was good to my mother when he and I were together. I asked Mick to buy her this little cottage called Yew Tree, and he did. Eva always blamed me for splitting up with Mick because after I left him we didn't have any money. She thought this was stupid.

I remember one funny scene with my mother while Mick and I were together. Some time in 1967, the three of us went to Ireland and stayed overnight with Desmond and Mariga Guinness at Leixlip Castle. Mariga put Eva in the King John Room, which was an enormous, ancient room with a copper bath. Eva had taken out her false teeth and popped them in a glass. Then she got into bed with her nightcap (a glass of whisky). Around 10.30 the door suddenly flew open and Mariga Guinness swept into the room like a great galleon followed by twenty-five Americans, all on a grand night-tour of the house. Mariga gestured around the room grandly saying, 'And this is the King John Room and here is Baroness Erisso reclining in King John's bed.' My poor mother was very upset. You can imagine how she felt – the poor thing. As grand as she was, she hated being on display. Mariga had presented her as some sort of rare old waxwork along with the rest of the antiques.

I, too, have an absolute horror of people 'dropping by'. I remember when I was living in the Shell Cottage. One afternoon Desmond turned up out of the blue with a party of Americans to give them a tour. Desmond somehow didn't understand my annoyance at all. He thought that bringing along a full picnic hamper for us all to have lunch would somehow make it fine. But for me it was a nightmare; I felt extremely uncomfortable with all these strangers picnicking outside my house. I guess this is what happens if you live in a house of historic significance; thank heavens I now live in blissful anonymity.

My mother's intrinsic feminism did not apply to my life in any way: my compromised situation during the Redlands bust, my difficulties as Mick's pop consort, my desire to establish my own identity at whatever cost. She didn't see the connection between her own bohemian youth and my own, and reacted especially badly to the Redlands bust. She couldn't see how we – Mick, Keith, Robert Fraser, and me – were all victims of police and political corruption. I know this sounds strange, but it always seemed that in her eyes I was *bad*. The fact that the press attacked us in the most vicious way, that the bust itself was a collusion between a sleazy tabloid and the police, not to mention

that the charges were specious and eventually thrown out –
none of this made any difference to her.

Parents, confronted with scandals involving their children, tend
to think, 'What are you doing? What were you thinking?! This
is absolutely beyond the pale.' Even my poor dad wasn't exactly
thrilled, I can tell you, but he understood it better. The Redlands
bust had an absolutely devastating effect on my mother. She was
honing her skills in teachers' training college when it happened,
and after that she left the college and started to sink into serious
depression and alcoholism. The shame – Mars bars and fur rugs
– was just too much for her. I'm sad to say I absorbed all this
negativity, not just my mother's of course, but *society's*, and
began a decline of my own. Perhaps I was telling my mother:
I'll see you one and raise you one.

While I was living on that wall in Soho where I spent my days
as a junkie, I would occasionally go home to Yew Tree to take a
bath and have a meal. Eva never said a thing. Did she know
what was going on? I don't think so. To begin with, she didn't
know I was using heroin. She eventually found that out when
I registered and was under Dr Willis's care, but all the time
on the wall? No, not really. Heroin was simply beyond her
ken. She knew I was up to no good, but she had no idea what
it was.

I'd lost Mick, I'd lost Nicholas, I'd lost everything that mattered
to me in life. I felt that I'd brought shame and disgrace on my
mother and I didn't know what to do. Living on the wall was
my way out of the life I was leading with Mick, which had

become unbearable to me. To me, the wall signified exit. But to my mother, my choice was simply incomprehensible and self-destructive, which it also was.

I was a very spoilt child, given pretty much what I wanted by my mother, and obviously she wanted something back, which I didn't give her. She wanted me to go to university, be a lady, and do well in life. Perhaps she had exaggerated expectations for me because her youth and ambitions had been thwarted, snatched away by the Second World War.

I don't honestly know what she expected me to become. She taught me to dance, and always made sure I had music lessons, piano lessons, singing lessons. I always assumed I was meant to make money or marry someone with money. What I never could get away from until quite recently was my role as a devoted daughter. I forgot to grow up.

Even with my son Nicholas, my mother took over completely. We had huge rows. I would say, '*I'm* the mother, not *you*. Take a back seat; he's *my* son!' But she couldn't. She had no idea that I could ever function as an adult – and I was never able to show her. Unlike many in my generation I *wanted* to grow up, and I think eventually I have – although some might argue the point.

I thought I would be able to hear Eva's stories go on forever – listening to her was like an oral history of her exotic aristocratic family, the Weimar Republic, the war – but in 1990 while I was away she became seriously ill with cancer and I returned to take care of her. I'm glad I did, because two years later she was gone.

Eva and I had many great times together. She loved mystery writers, gardening and films, especially about the circus – odd that, but she was a dancer and liked to see athletic people doing athletic things. She could be a lot of fun and I could talk to her like a sister. Another thing: I always felt like she was drinking me in, and it's hard to get that feeling again with anyone else.

Eva kept her mind to the very end. She stayed sharp, funny, intransigent and enchanting – all the things she was. A very odd thing, after she died Yew Tree Cottage began to crumble. When I was last there, it seemed that if you even leaned against the house it was going to fall to pieces. Eva and Yew Tree had grown into each other, and when she was gone it too gave up the ghost.

my weimar period

I think I must have the Weimar Republic in my DNA. That night world of intellectual cabarets – Kurt Weill and Bertolt Brecht – and *Neue Sachlichkeit* painters – George Grosz and Otto Dix – which fell asleep in my mother and woke up in me. In the early 1930s in Berlin the playwright Bertolt Brecht and the composer Kurt Weill collaborated on a series of brilliant, edgy musicals, the best-known of which is *The Threepenny Opera*, and in my imagination I entered their haunted world. I did *The Seven Deadly Sins* very much *for* my mother. I wish that she'd been alive to see it.

I originally got into my Weimar period – *20th Century Blues*, *The Seven Deadly Sins* (and you might include *Vagabond Ways* in this group) – through my friend and long-time collaborator, Hal Willner. Hal played me the Brecht/Weill song-cycle *The Seven Deadly Sins*, I listened to the record and read the text and realised that I *had* to do it. That reanimated my interest in their music.

The idea of creating a performance around Weill's music first occurred to me when I was doing a concert at the Brooklyn

Academy of Music: twentieth-century decadent music featuring Hindemith, Gershwin, Brecht and Weill. That concert was the beginning of the concept of *An Evening in the Weimar Republic with Marianne Faithfull* as a cabaret. Then in 1985 I performed the Brecht/Weill song, 'The Ballad of the Soldier's Wife' in Hal Willner and Paul M. Young's production of *Lost in the Stars: The Music of Kurt Weill*.

I then played Jenny in *The Threepenny Opera* in Dublin at the Gate Theatre in 1992 for two months. Playing Jenny was an incredibly charged experience and got me right into it. 'Pirate Jenny' is one of the great revenge songs of all time. Jenny is a prostitute and a waitress in a shitty hotel on the docks, her pimp is Macheath, famous from 'Mack the Knife'. Jenny has an apocalyptic and grisly fantasy of what she will do to those who have oppressed and humiliated her when the ominous black ship comes into port to exact its revenge.

> *And they'll say, 'Well, which ones shall we kill?'*
> *They'll say, 'Which ones shall we kill?'*
> *Come the dot of twelve, it will be still in the harbour,*
> *When they ask me, 'Well, who is going to die?'*
> *And you'll hear me whispering, oh, so sweetly, 'All of them!'*
> *And as the soft heads fall, I'll say, 'Hop-là!'*

I sang 'Salomon's Song' every night. It's about powerful men and pimps (and a whorish queen) and what they do with their power. It was just after Gorbachev and Glasnost and the breaking down of the Soviet Union. Every night when I sang, a fresh bit of news would have come out and the song would have a slightly different meaning.

> *How great and wise was Salomon!*
> *Watch out the world is spinning fast*
> *The night will fall, the price we'll pay*
> *Such wisdom's not all it's cracked up to be,*
> *So let us praise such clarity.*

———————————

In 1995, I began to choose songs for a cabaret performance called *An Evening in the Weimar Republic*. It was a lot of work and in another style entirely from my usual repertoire, so, thank God, we had a lot of help from my piano player, the brilliant Paul Trueblood.

I took *An Evening in the Weimar Republic* on the road and it was picked up as an album by BMG. The CD was called *20th Century Blues* because I sing Noel Coward and other songs on it not by Kurt Weill and because it came out right at the end of the twentieth century. It was a cabaret act we recorded live in a jazz club in Paris on a shoestring.

Unfortunately, an awful thing happened right at the beginning of the *Weimar Republic* tour. I walked off the stage – literally – and into the front row. I used to open up with 'Moon of Alabama' looking up at the spotlight, which represented the moon. That night I came on and walked straight off the edge of the stage, landed on my coccyx, and cracked it. So for the rest of the tour I was in agony. I didn't take any painkillers for it; I just had to cope. It was a stupid accident: I wasn't drunk, I wasn't high. Now we put a white line on the edge of the stage.

And while doing *An Evening in the Weimar Republic* I realised that this was the way to *get* to *The Seven Deadly Sins*. Something I'd been wanting to do for years, ever since Hal Willner played it for me. I wouldn't call *20th Century Blues* easy exactly, but it was a lot easier to do than *The Seven Deadly Sins*; *20th Century Blues* is a medley, *The Seven Deadly Sins* is an opera/ballet in the formidable Brecht/Weill canon.

The Seven Deadly Sins was originally a 'ballet song-cycle'. The story is very simple: Anna is sent by her family to make money by dancing so that the family can build their dream house in Louisiana. She sets off on her journey through seven American cities, but the pressure of having to make money and resist her own carnal temptations is too much for her and she splits into two characters. Anna I (the singer) is the sensible, goal-oriented one, determined to fulfil her family's demands. Anna II (the dancer) is constantly being led astray by her own desires and has to be restrained by the admonitions of Anna I. The sister who's singing is the one wagging the finger all the time, and the sister who's dancing is the one going through the experiences, but all ends happily, you'll be glad to hear, and the family gets their dream house.

After their many famous collaborations during the Weimar Republic – *The Threepenny Opera, The Rise and Fall of the City of Mahagonny* – *The Seven Deadly Sins* would be the last time

Kurt Weill and Bertolt Brecht worked together. The original production was mounted in Paris in 1933 and financed by the wealthy English eccentric Edward James on the condition that his wife, the dancer Tilly Losch, would have a leading role in the production. Lotte Lenya sang the part of Anna I. Tilly Losch danced the part of Anna II. Lotte and Tilly ended up having a passionate love affair and everybody got very upset.

It wasn't easy to get permission from the Kurt Weill Foundation to perform *The Seven Deadly Sins*. I had to go there with Jason Osborne, my first conductor, and show them I wasn't some sort of bimbo, some idiot, and that I really understood what it was about and that I was prepared to go the whole way. And I did. The Weill Foundation won't let you perform it unless you use a fifty-nine-piece orchestra. Although it's something I wasn't used to, it was absolutely wonderful working with a full orchestra.

I first did *The Seven Deadly Sins* with Jason Osborne at St Ann's in Brooklyn, and for years I would do it live wherever I could. But it was only when I started working with the conductor Dennis Russell Davies that I realised we could actually record this. Dennis was heaven to work with and saved my bacon so many times. He had been involved in both the BAM concerts and also worked with me and my band. 'Dennis,' I said, 'we've got through *20th Century Blues* intact, what would you say to taking on *The Seven Deadly Sins*?' To which – to my intense relief – he said, 'Yes, that's a *great* idea; let's do it.'

Brecht's lyrics for *The Seven Deadly Sins* are deeply ironic;
the entire libretto is in the form of a looking-glass morality.
What he's done is take the seven deadly sins and turn them on
their head. They're no longer the seven deadly sins; they're the
seven deadly *virtues*. Lust becomes love, anger becomes
righteous anger at the dull stupid people in LA, rage at their
cruelty.

> *If you take offence at injustice,*
> *Mister Big will show he's offended;*
> *If a curse or a blow can enrage you so*
> *Your usefulness here is ended.*

The lyrics can be very funny, as in the Gluttony scene where
they weigh Anna every single day. She's got a job, and she
mustn't put on weight – gaining half an ounce means trouble.
It's in her contract. That's so modern!

> *Her contract has been signed to do a solo turn,*
> *It forbids her ever eating when or what she likes to eat,*
> *She likes to eat, she likes to eat.*

I so understood this, I can't tell you. And the whole business
where she's misguidedly developed pride in her work – talking
about cabaret as art – and doesn't seem to realise that's not what
people come to a cabaret for . . . they want tits and arse.

The really interesting scenario is Lust, where Anna I lectures
Anna II about her love life. Anna II is meant to be going after a
rich man but falls in love with this guy Fernando, who's

penniless. Anna I sends him off, but I think there is an intimation that she has a bit of a scene with him herself, in the song, and at the very end Anna II poignantly says, 'It's right like this, Anna, but so hard!' I play both Annas, of course, and I naturally relate to the themes personally; in popular mythology I'm associated with quite a few of the seven deadly sins.

The Seven Deadly Sins was not that well known until Lotte Lenya recorded it in the fifties, but by then she was fifty-seven and her voice was no longer the soprano with which she'd originally sung it so they had to adjust the music. My voice is no longer a soprano, either, and I sing it an octave lower. Lotte Lenya and I both developed these smoky, whisky voices later in life. If there are overtones or undertones of Lotte Lenya in my voice, you know, it's probably because I was listening to Lotte Lenya in my mother's womb.

We recorded *The Seven Deadly Sins* in June 1997 at the Konzerthaus in Vienna with Dennis Russell Davies conducting the Vienna Radio Symphony Orchestra. On the album there are a few extra Brecht/Weill songs because *The Seven Deadly Sins* itself is only forty-five minutes long – the additional songs were also beautifully orchestrated.

The Seven Deadly Sins is my favourite record. It has very personal resonances for me. I was performing it in Brisbane when my mother died – and recording it when my father died. That's why I dedicated it to my parents.

I wanted to do *An Evening in the Weimar Republic with Marianne Faithfull*, and then I wanted to do *The Seven Deadly Sins* and stop. But of course what the record company thought was, 'Oh, now she can do Jacques Brel and become a cabaret artist with an endless repertoire.' They thought I was going to turn into Rod Stewart and do all the old standards – and, of course, he's making a fortune. But I'd already done a bit of that on *Strange Weather*. I might actually some day do a bit more! But I didn't want to be put on some old-standards assembly-line, so that's why my next album, *Vagabond Ways,* turned out to be so defiant.

me and the fabulous beast

The Fabulous Beast has a life of its own. It goes to parties I
never attended, it has affairs with people I've never met, it
snorts coke, misbehaves and says outrageous things in the press.
And everybody's so *interested* in the Fabulous Beast: her whereabouts, her habits, all that naughty-unicorn-of-rock-infamy
stuff.

A few years ago I was leaving a reception at the Massachusetts
Institute of Technology and noticed a list of the people
attending, saying who they were and what they did. I was down
as 'Marianne Faithfull – Legend'. Naturally, I was quite
pleased. The perks are fabulous, of course, and I am so *very*
good at taking advantage of them. That's why I am always
surprised when I come up against that double-edged sword; in
fact, the whole fame bit has a very nasty side to it – a side over
which I have no control.

Fabulous Beast: Boo-hoo.

Oh dear, the Fabulous Beast doesn't like whingeing. Doesn't like it when I go on about people's weird perceptions of me. But I still believe people love to witness destruction and drugs.

Fabulous Beast: And God knows I've done both spectacularly!

But just think what I might have become if my mother hadn't sold me to Andrew Oldham at seventeen!

Fabulous Beast: Oh, what nonsense, Marianne! At seventeen you're an adult. People have been rulers of France at sixteen.

Oh, I know, I know, darling, like Marie Antoinette, but you're not *actually* an adult. *She* certainly wasn't an adult, in case you haven't seen the film.

Fabulous Beast: Listen, the Black Prince won the Battle of Crécy at sixteen.

That's just boys' games. Defeating the French army was nothing compared to Andrew Loog Oldham.

Fabulous Beast: Who are you kidding? Let's face it, you'd be nothing without Andrew or me, baby.

Oh, I'm meant to be grateful, now, too? For a life of humiliation, slander, the butt of dirty jokes . . .

Fabulous Beast: Price of fame, darling, price of fame.

It would have been much better if I had finished school and gone to university –

Fabulous Beast: Oh, puhleeze! Meeting Sir Andrew was the beginning of our fabulous career together, our legend.

Well, it was the beginning of your career, not mine! Fuck the legend.

Fabulous Beast: Many have.

That's just an urban myth. Once your persona becomes a fixture in the press, it starts living its own life. I've tried killing it off by generating an even more lethal version of myself, but this naturally creates *other* problems; plus, the original caricature lives on regardless. Over the years a lurid parade of Mariannes has appeared and now they all exist simultaneously.

Fabulous Beast: First, there was the Virgin on the Pedestal . . .

Shut up, I'm trying to remember what comes next. Oh yes, the Girl-in-the-Fur-Rug of the Redlands bust, also known as the Bad-Mother-who-leaves-her-husband-and-child-and-runs-away-with-Mick-Jagger.

Fabulous Beast: I had nothing to do with that.

Can you be serious for a minute? What do you think a nineteen-year-old girl who is being kept as some sort of angel on a pedestal would want to do?

Fabulous Beast: Go wild! She wants to smash it, and so I did. I think I might have gone a little too far. On the other hand, I had a lot of fun doing it.

Unfortunately in the process a sort of shadow Marianne materialised, this Other that has nothing to do with me and is not in my movie.

Fabulous Beast: I hope you're not talking about me.

Well, maybe I was, but can you blame me? Miss X, nude in a fur rug and all that. People are so smitten with the naughty bits they forget there was a happy – but brief – domestic bit with Mick. We were in heaven. I'm amazed at how fast it all went. There was the bust and my miscarriage when I was with Mick and the baby I lost and how it haunts me. And, of course, I've always felt it was my fault.

Fabulous Beast: You're too hard on yourself.

Hmm . . .

Fabulous Beast: I'm kidding.

The truth is I was hardly taking any drugs at all.

Fabulous Beast: Hardly any drugs? Isn't that like a little bit pregnant?

When I got pregnant, I'd deliberately gone to Ireland with Nicholas and my mother to stay away from all that and the turmoil around the making of *Performance*. It all went well while I was in Ireland and only when I got back to London and then my waters broke did the problems start – it was terribly traumatic. That's when the naughty wench in the fur rug morphed into something far more sinister.

> *Fabulous Beast: Good! I was getting bored with those two corny incarnations: Devil or Angel? Makes one want to burst into song. And if I'm not mistaken, your next incarnation came from a song – THAT song.*

Yes, 'Sister Morphine' was the beginning of a misunderstanding: the idea that everything that I write or sing about is autobiographical.

> *Fabulous Beast: I think I may have started that rubbish myself.*

Writing about myself all the time would bore me to death. In any case, 'Sister Morphine' was written before I ever took morphine. It's a *story*. I made it up, as I've been saying for years, but people will believe what they want to believe.

> *Well, it just goes to show*
> *Things are not what they seem*
> *Please, Sister Morphine, turn my nightmares into dreams*
> *Oh, can't you see I'm fading fast?*
> *And that this shot will be my last*

Marie Antoinette and I have a similar problem in that regard – people still believe to this day the lies and the libels that were written about her.

Fabulous Beast: The apple doesn't fall far from the tree, Maria Teresa.

I'm beginning to realise that there is nothing I can do about it. All I can say is that, after writing 'Sister Morphine', I learned that you must be very careful what you write about because – it may come true! Years later I wrote a song called 'Demon Lover'. I remembered the lesson of 'Sister Morphine' and I've never released it.

Fabulous Beast: Hey, I thought I was your demon lover.

Don't tell me you're jealous?

Fabulous Beast: That's part of my job description. Speaking of which, I'd love to hear what else you're going to blame me for. Probably your drug addiction.

Well, it just so happens that the Girl-on-the-Wall was my next incarnation. People just assume I was selling my body for drugs. How else would I have been able to support my habit? The actual story is far more interesting: on the wall I found not degradation but the goodness of humanity.

Fabulous Beast: I would hardly call that more interesting.

How dare you? I ran up £20,000 in drug bills. People gave me things. They looked after me. The Chinese restaurant let me wash my clothes, Gypsy looked after me and even the cops watched over me. All this has been turned into Marianne Faithfull on heroin and on the game.

Fabulous Beast: Come on, stop romanticising the wall. Talk about creating legends.

You flatter me. I would have been happy just disappearing into that wall.

Fabulous Beast: But, sweetheart, with that voice and that presence, what else could you have been but a diva?

Actually, my voice was never that good.

Fabulous Beast: Then why didn't you just stay on the goddamn wall? But no, you had to go out and . . . What? Go back to college? Help the poor? Become a teacher? No, you had to go and . . . make a record. Case closed.

Hmm, that would be the punky, junkie *Broken English* Marianne you're talking about? That was a complete shock to all concerned – including me. Most people didn't know what had become of me. Or care. Sob!

Fabulous Beast: I may need a drink and a line of blow to get through this.

Just before *Broken English*, I honestly believed that I was going to die, but I felt strongly that before I died I had to reveal myself as I was at that time. And that's how *Broken English* came about. That's a long time ago now. Of course, I'm not that person any more, and I never will be again. I fully expected to drop dead.

Fabulous Beast: Yes, you've made that quite clear.

I had thought it would be a simple matter, but it was harder than I imagined.

Fabulous Beast: Ah! Even harder for me.

Oh, you'll never die. No use even trying. But, back to *my* life, if you don't mind. Me being me, I decided it was time for a change. In 1988 I moved to Dublin and began to feel, you know, wanted. 'Dreaming My Dreams' went to number 1 in Ireland. I realised I still had something to say.

Fabulous Beast: The Irish are very forgiving, you know. And, of course, anyone whom the English hate, the Irish welcome with open arms!

After I wrote my autobiography I realised I had feelings that I hadn't put in the book. I had got into the habit of memory – and it *is* a habit – and I was left with all these floating images, things that were not really stories or anything I could put into words. Just feelings, and so I put them into my album, *Vagabond Ways*, which came out in 1999. *Vagabond Ways* is my line in the sand, really. I didn't even know I was doing it. I thought I was writing 'The End' to the Book of Marianne. But, of course, when 2000 rolled around, I thought to myself, Who am I going to be next?

> *Fabulous Beast: You see? I told you, you can't just live like other people. Does Mrs Brenda Barnacle of 147 Old Kent Road wonder who she's going to be next?*

On the whole, to keep my sanity I have to avoid thinking too much about the shadow, the public's idea of me.

> *Fabulous Beast: But we admire many of our old heroes precisely because they lived such wild lives: François Villon, Caravaggio, Byron, Rimbaud, John Wilmot, Earl of Rochester – one of my faves – and even our Keith –*

Well, I do have a desire to please sometimes, and there have been occasions against my better judgement when I thought I was obliged to act out the creature.

> *Fabulous Beast: But, darling, what could be better than swanning into the room in full sail in front of people, strutting one's stuff . . .*

Well, it is not a pretty sight. Plus, it's not good for my character or my health.

> *Fabulous Beast [declaiming]: The play's the thing wherein we'll catch the conscience of the king.*

If I don't get it out onstage, I just end up sucking all the oxygen out of the room, like a monster! I end up not liking myself. I want to avoid the trap that Janis and so many other people fell into, where the lines get blurred, and you no longer know what's you, what's your persona, what's on stage, what's offstage. Janis died of it, in fact.

Fabulous Beast: But that's what makes us so interesting!

Don't be absurd. Now, where was I? I'm quite short but . . . once I begin performing, this odd thing happens: I physically seem to grow on stage – people think I'm tall! But back in my dressing room, you'll find this wuzzly little person.

Fabulous Beast: Well, as Maria Teresa in Marie Antoinette, *you did seem a bit larger than life. I don't think anyone would disagree with that.*

The music biz is fixated on celebrity. It's bloody pathological. All those reality shows on television give me the complete *horrors*. The idea that, in your private life, there would be a camera and crew filming you!

Fabulous Beast: Well, how can you blame them – they're trying to get in touch with their own Fabulous Beast.

You would say that! Thanks to you – you slut! you dope addict! – I am the Marianne Faithfull of tabloids, salacious journalists, smutty-minded cops. I find myself joined with you at the hip, for better or worse . . .

Fabulous Beast: For richer or poorer . . .

Don't remind me! The reason I live in Ireland is because nobody here could be remotely bothered to feed the Fabulous Beast. Nobody gives a toss about that here.

Fabulous Beast: Some gratitude! Marianne, I know you, I am you, and I happen to know you are much more ambitious than that!

Well, I certainly was very ambitious, but I think it could have waited.

Fabulous Beast: But you wouldn't have been a pop singer, you wouldn't have met the Rolling Stones . . . Don't you know one only regrets the things one didn't do. I mean, if you hadn't done that, you'd probably be telling me now, 'If only I'd –'

This is exhausting. I think I'll take a nap.

stealing coal

I was thinking about Ireland in a dreamy, desultory sort of way when one of those mortifying scenes of one's bad behaviour – and I have more than most – popped into my mind.

I was living in Wicklow. It was a particularly cold winter that year, and one evening, whilst staying in the film director John Boorman's cottage as his guest, I did a very naughty thing. I should have been buying my own coal but I didn't and I had just run out and the fire was beginning to die. Well, I knew where John and Isabella kept their coal in the yard, so I crept into the bunker with my rubber gloves and scuttle only to be caught red- or should I say black-handed by John. Very, very embarrassing. I know John laughs about this now, but at the time I'm sure he was justifiably piqued. Of course, I was caught and that was that; there was absolutely no way I could wriggle out of it! And, you know, in Ireland fuel is sacred; it's like water in rural France. If you know Marcel Pagnol's *Manon des Sources* you'll understand what I mean. People would fight and die over water in parts of France. In Ireland, it's fuel.

And then, to compound it, Anita Pallenberg came to stay with me at the cottage. She had just had an operation on her back and needed some rest away from the hurly-burly of London. And so it happened that one bitter evening we ran out of coal for the fire, so I sent poor Anita up to John's coal bunker with the scuttle. Did I tell her the story or warn her of the dangers? Well, that would have made no sense; she wouldn't have gone.

Of course she was caught immediately, and horribly shocked. John wasn't cross – he was gobsmacked, absolutely astonished: astonished that I would send my poor, innocent friend who was recovering from a back injury out to nick coal from his bunker. I know for a fact that he's dined out many a time on that story, and so have I.

uncle bill & auntie allen: down among the beats at the jack kerouac school of disembodied poetics

What do Beat writers eat for breakfast? Not, as you might imagine, peyote buttons and Gallo Hearty Burgundy. In the mornings, my friend, the writer Deborah Theodore and I would go down to Allen Ginsberg's apartment and have porridge with him. It was all part of Allen having a very delicate constitution, you see, he had to be very careful what he ate. Whereas when I had breakfast with Bill Burroughs, I didn't get breakfast, *Bill* had breakfast. Some of my fondest memories of Allen, Auntie Allen, are of him just cooking in his kitchen.

> From Deb's journal:
> Allen invited us over for oatmeal with [the poet] Carl Rakosi. What a mess of stuff he (AG) added to his oatmeal – Bonito flakes and seaweed and sesame and fermented barley and pine nuts. That boy needs a mother!

For three summers I taught at the Jack Kerouac School of Disembodied Poetics aka the Naropa Institute in Boulder, Colorado. Allen Ginsberg had founded it in 1975 along with

Chögyam Trungpa Rinpoche, a Buddhist sage whom he'd met during a dispute over a taxi.

The Jack Kerouac School of Disembodied Poetics was a nutty place run on exquisitely nutty lines and originally overseen by the Beat Holy Trinity: Allen Ginsberg, William Burroughs and Gregory Corso. Gregory had gone by the time I got there, but his infamous behaviour was still the stuff of legend. The three of them at their most outrageous, and running a school! School for scandal – definitely! Allen, too. Allen tried to seduce his students. It was just outrageous, the whole thing – but you would expect no less from the Beat academy of advanced underground studies. The Jack Kerouac School of Disembodied Poetics was joined at the hip – or *by* hip – to the Naropa Institute, which was overseen by the equally outrageous Chögyam Trungpa Rinpoche.

By the time I got to Naropa, Trungpa was dead, which I think was rather a good thing in Allen's case, because Allen had been inhibited by him. Trungpa told Allen to shave off his beard and he did; Trungpa told Allen that he was too in love with his fame and Allen shrank. And, of course, those incredible scenes with Trungpa – he was just crazy . . . and drunk. There's all these wild stories!

Having read all Trungpa Rinpoche's books I thought his message basically was: the great demon is the ego. I remember when I asked Allen about it, he said, 'Listen, as an artist you cannot work without your ego.' So, he must have come to terms with the whole thing. 'No,' Allen continued, 'the ego is not the villain. It's part of you and you *need* it. It's like an arm or a leg. It's just as important. You don't want to let it run riot – but you don't have to get rid of it, either.' And that's what I'm trying to do, to rein it in a bit – at least for today!

I was very attracted to meditation and so was Deb:

> Meditation is simple instruction for complicated animals. I sit and my mind is cluttered with all my stuff. I greet my thoughts, thank you, and breathe out. It's like being on a reception line for an endless number of guests: Hello, Nice to see you, Thank you, How's the family? Nice dress, oh, See you again.

Meditation instructor Barbara Dufty says that Buddhism without meditation is like the difference between looking at an apple and eating it. I got the hang of it, and slowing down the brain and the metabolism does let you focus on the tiniest detail and see it as a conundrum of existence:

> Meanwhile, I 'sat' another whole hour today as a fly walked my face up my inanimate arm and several tears ran down my face, from what emotion I could not imagine ... The fly crawling up as the tear rolled down. Both the same. Equally oblivious to both – which was which?
> (From Deb's journal)

The first year I went to the Jack Kerouac School I had to go through an interview process where Allen and the poet Larry Fagin grilled me. Allen really wanted me there, but all the rest of them put me through my paces, I had to jump through hoops for them to show I really was up to snuff. The interviews went like this: Did I know *Middlemarch*? Had I read Geoffrey Chaucer? Did I know Shakespeare? And I did! I thought they were going to ask me to quote from *Les Chants de Maldoror* or Rimbaud. I thought it was going to be, like, heavy, underground stuff, but most of the questions were about the classics, the European canon. I really went through it on charm. As I do. Sliding through life on charm! They couldn't tell me 'no', and of course, I had Allen backing me up to the hilt.

I've always felt a little insecure about my education. Like Gregory I was – what's the word? – an autodidact. I didn't have what you'd call 'a good education'. I went through a very good school but, not going to university, didn't absorb all that stuff you learn as a matter of course. I went to the University of Life, as it were, and I wouldn't change that (not that I have any choice). At Naropa there was a wonderful moment when Allen gave me a little medal which said: 'MARIANNE FAITHFULL – PROFESSOR OF POETICS' with 'JACK KEROUAC SCHOOL OF DISEMBODIED POETICS' on the back. That was the greatest! Better than any honorary degree, isn't it? And then, one of the funniest things he did was correct my book. Any quotations I got wrong, and apparently there were a few, Allen corrected. He corrected them all.

'The proper Ancient Greek name for the promontory of Attica is "Cape Sunion",' Allen pointed out, '*not* "Cape Sunium". Sunium is the old Latin name which no one uses any more. It sounds fustian and vaguely imperialist, like two old Etonians eating their cucumber sandwiches on the steps of the Temple to Poseidon.'

There was some wonderful quote from Milton that I apparently got wrong, Allen admonishing me with a line from Lord Byron, *'with just enough learning to misquote'*. But did I really say I'd used Milton's *Lycidas* as the model for 'Sister Morphine'? *'Yet once more, O ye laurels, and once more/Ye Myrtles brown, with ivy never sere/I come to pluck your berries harsh and crude.'* That *Lycidas*? Well, it *was* an elegy, wasn't it? (even if for someone old Milton barely knew). And 'Sister Morphine' was an elegy, too, wasn't it? Anyway, Allen, the great list-maker, Sublime Accountant of Poesie, schoolmaster manqué, found all my mistakes in that book. *Tiny* mistakes. Professor Ginzy caught them all. You minded when your editor corrected you, you minded when your friends pointed out mistakes, but you didn't mind with Allen. Of course not.

At Naropa I taught songwriting. Lyric writing, actually. I just did what Gregory did, I winged it! I tried to find what was *in* people and bring it *out*. Did I produce any notable students from that? I don't know! It was hard, because they all connected me with – Mick Jagger! God! I've got over this now – I have, haven't I? – but there was a time when I *really* didn't want to be lumped in with the Stones and Mick Jagger. I've got over it, definitely, but what, you may ask, did Mick & Co. have to do with my teaching? Nothing. I wasn't teaching the *Rolling Stones Songbook* of drugs, delinquency, and the lower depths. But that's what they saw me as: the Stones' rock'n'roll moll.

That's not what Allen saw and it's not what William saw and it's not what Gregory saw, but it's what students saw – a rock wench who *also* wrote songs.

I just read this note in Deb's journal:

> Marianne's workshop on writing: 'THINGS TAKE TIME'. Write it, put it away, don't judge it.

So me! Anything to put off the moment – even if this approach does have the classic endorsement of Wordsworth & Co. *'Emotion recollected in tranquillity'* and so on. Never mind that Bob Dylan, Van Morrison, and Beck write their lyrics as the band is tuning up – and Eminem and Jay-Z forego even that, just rapping out their great wild rhymes *while* the track is playing. Well, we each have our own methods, don't we?

Needless to say, at the Jack Kerouac School there were lots of very earnest, brow-wrinkling poets reading very meaningful verse in excruciatingly meaningful voices. The awkwardness of putting one's deepest, most private thoughts on public display is always a bit daunting. Deb captures the anxiety perfectly:

> Surrounded by poets reading from notebooks. I write with the knowledge of possibly being read out loud – by me, a traitor to my own privacy. Maybe this poet life is just too rich for me. Probably it is. But I would like to break on through to the other side before I quit.

I don't come from that period of time where we thought of ourselves as self-conscious artists, much as we would have liked to. Art for me has to be a craft. I'm still a bit like that. I think it's a good place to start from. Because you can really get up your own arse if you start thinking you're a poet – unless you really *are* a poet. Even Allen went through a lot of hassle wanting to be so famous and wanting to be the best poet and yet knowing William was such a great writer and such a great *lyric* writer, too, not as in writing song lyrics, but a writer of great lyrical passages. And in the end, that's where I stand with William. Once you know what great lyrical imagination is, you can't go anywhere else.

> Death rows the boy like sleeping marble down the Grand Canal in a gondola of gold and crystal . . . poles out into a vast lagoon: souvenir postcards and bronzed baby shoes, Grand Canyon and Niagara Falls, Chimborazo, New York skyline and Aztec pyramid. Pinks and blues and yellows of religious objects in the Catholic store on a red-brick square surrounded by trees.
>
> WILLIAM S. BURROUGHS, from 'Word' in *Interzone*

I've learnt so much from his writing, especially his later books, *The Western Lands* and those books. I love them. I no longer find off-putting the endless sex scenes with boys, maybe that's because I'm a woman. I just don't care. Skip them! There's so many parts in it that are just beautiful. It's like I was saying about the Beats in general; whatever their flaws, there are these parts that are so worth it, that outweigh the parts that aren't worth it. Not too many of those, anyway.

When I got to Naropa I told Burroughs there was something I wanted to ask him. He must have known what was coming a bit, but being a real mensch, he said: 'Okay, I'll see you at eight thirty tomorrow morning.'

Bill was very resistant to me in the sixties – to put it mildly! – because I really wasn't formed and I was just a pretty, silly little girl with nothing to say. He could be very rude to women. It was just astonishing how he'd treat women like morons – people he'd never met before. But, that's how he acted! What can you say? Burroughs knew, because his wife Joan was no fool, that women weren't *all* like that, but when he got to me he couldn't see there was anything else there. Things changed somewhat when I went to sing at the Kansas Poetry Festival – it was put on *for* William really. I sang 'Times Square' and won his heart. He began to see, I suppose, from my songs that there was more to me than this blonde who had got hooked up with Mick Jagger.

Little did he know that I'd been an apt pupil of his – too apt, as it turned out – for many years. I didn't just *fall* into the junkie life, I'd made a *study* of it. I took it straight out of William Burroughs's *Naked Lunch* actually. I took it absolutely literally. Chapter and verse. The Beat mythology of heroin use. A light bulb went on in my head when I read *Naked Lunch*. I realised, any time you want to escape this world, this is what you do: you go out and become a junkie and live on the street. Of course, what I did *not* know was that you can't play around with heroin. Heroin is as close as you'll ever get to death while you're still living. When I made this plan to disappear into the rabbit hole of heroin I thought that I could drop out and drop in again. I had no idea that it would take two years to do my little junkie experiment and then another fifteen to get off, you see. Now I have people fantasising about *me* with a needle in my arm, just as I fantasised about the junkie life from William Burroughs's books. Either you think you're king of the world or complete slime. I have a tendency in this direction.

So at eight thirty, I turned up at Bill's room. He was having a boiled egg with soldiers – the one meal he could cook for himself – and what I wanted to ask him was: Why? Why did that happen to me? Why when I read *Naked Lunch* did I decide that it said 'EXIT'? And it worked! But obviously, I didn't really understand yet, and Bill, speaking in his slow drawl, very gently said, 'Ya know, Marianne, you might have just taken it a bit *too far*, but if that's what you *felt* you had to do, then you had to do that. That is the road and only the person on the road knows how far it goes. It might lead you to Timbuktu, it might lead you to Avenue B . . . or the Interzone.'

I quoted a line I recalled from *Naked Lunch*. 'Junk is not like alcohol or weed, a means to increased enjoyment of life. Junk is not a kick. It is a way of life.'

'But, my dear, I was just stating the facts. I'm not in the business of giving advice.'

'Well,' I said, 'maybe I read between the lines a bit.'

Burroughs had got into his heroin addiction by accident, when his friend Herbert Huncke ('the world's oldest junkie,' as he used to bill himself) scored some ampoules of morphine, which is why he was always sceptical about people falling in love with the romance of heroin. 'The big mistake Keith Richards made,' he said, 'was that he thought it would make him immortal. Heroin doesn't make you immortal, it only makes you improbable.'

I thought that was heaven, Williams Burroughs talking so seriously about being my spiritual-Zen-drug godfather, whilst eating a boiled egg with soldiers. I loved William very much. He was so kind that day, and so compassionate. I can't believe he didn't just say, 'Get the fuck out of here, you stupid little twit!'

After I'd been at Naropa a while Allen came to my room and sat down and had a little chat with me. I was not fulfilling my duties.

'Marianne, you're falling down on your job! You're letting me down here!'

'Oh, and what's that, Allen?'

'One of the things you're expected to do here is shag the students!' (There was some girl apparently who was in love with me but I just didn't want to make it with her.)

'You're kidding me!'

'No, I'm not!' He wasn't.

This was apparently part of the curriculum, one of the requirements of the faculty! You can imagine that on the prospectus: 'Come to the Jack Kerouac School and get fucked!' That's how outrageously anti-bourgey it was. The diametric opposite of every other learning institution on earth. At most colleges people get fired for fucking their students! The very outrageousness of the Jack Kerouac School was what many of the students found attractive. I think one of the reasons Deb liked being there was that her parents *couldn't bear* Allen Ginsberg!

I told Allen I didn't want to and I wasn't going to, and if that's what they got me there for, tough shit! That was my attitude. It didn't even occur to me that sleeping with the students was expected of me! I'm the child of two very good teachers, and I know a lot about this sleeping with students business. It's very dangerous. A very bad idea; it's like child abuse almost. It's getting someone's trust and then misusing it.

Actually, Burroughs wasn't trying to fuck his students, either. I know he's famous for saying the only reason for teaching is to have sex with your students, but, as we know, he was given to saying all kinds of stuff he didn't necessarily follow up on. The last thing he wanted to do was fuck the students.

I went to all Allen's Walt Whitman courses and his Blake courses. I learnt a lot. I didn't know Whitman at all, so for me it was a revelation. And obviously Allen would immediately go in for the homoerotic quality in Whitman. Allen, with great relish, pointed out the irony that in his own time Whitman was threatened with prosecution not for the overtly homosexual Calamus poems in *Leaves of Grass*, but for his heterosexual love poems.

It was Allen who introduced me to the cosmic, long-breath ecstasies of Whitman, his almost lascivious embrace of nature:

> *I am the poet of the woman same as the man . . .*
> *I am he that walks with the tender and growing night.*
> *I call to the earth and sea half-held by the night.*
> *Press close bare-bosom'd night – press close magnetic nourishing*
> *   night!*
> *Night of south winds – night of the large few stars!*
> *Still nodding night – mad naked summer night.*

Unfortunately, I was so un-self-aware that I didn't realise how amazing it was! I just didn't know! And all the readings he gave of his late poems, which I don't know if people really appreciate as much as they should – the ones about,

> *Now I lie alone and a youth*
> *Stalks my house, he won't in truth*
> *Come to bed with me, instead*
> *Loves the thoughts inside my head.*

– all that stuff. Allen's insecurity. He was so lovable, really lovable, and God damn it, gone!

Bill was there teaching his nutty stuff. I sat through some of Bill's classes, but I can't remember too much about them. He was so perverse. All about Raudive recordings where you could hear voices on a tape recorded in an empty room, Kirlian photography, Reichian Orgone boxes.

In *When I Was Cool*, Sam Kashner's account of his summer at Naropa, a student interrupts Burroughs's rant about receiving messages from inanimate objects like refrigerators and steam pipes by asking, 'Isn't it only crazy people who think that the television is talking to them?' Burroughs responds to the question with the Möbius-strip logic of one of his tautological fables:

> Some time ago, a young man came to see me. And said he was going mad. Street signs, overheard conversations, radio broadcasts seemed to refer to him in some way. I told him, 'Of course they refer to you. You see them and you hear them.'

I was always surprised that Bill took these crank ideas so literally, especially from someone who had such a sharp, clear-eyed view of the world. Some of the Sayings of Chairman Bill:

> Desperation is the raw material of drastic change. Only those who can leave behind everything they have ever believed in can hope to escape.

> After a shooting spree, they always want to take the guns away from the people who didn't do it. I sure as hell

wouldn't want to live in a society where the only people allowed guns are the police and the military.

Most of the trouble in this world has been caused by folks who can't mind their own business, because they have no business of their own to mind, any more than a smallpox virus has.

There couldn't be a society of people who didn't dream. They'd be dead in two weeks.

———————

The second year at Naropa I went with my friend the producer, Hal Willner. That's when Hal got the idea to record Allen and William, and that's how he met them. And I'm very glad that I was able to facilitate that, because it meant a lot to Allen – the wonderful *Holy Soul Jelly Roll* box set Hal produced for him. I don't think Bill cared. But he did do a great job on Bill's record, *Dead City Radio*.

Billy Junior, Burroughs's son, was dead by the time I got to Naropa. The hardest thing for me to deal with was the heartlessness of Bill. I knew all about the battle story of Billy Junior. It was all over and rationalised by the time I came along, but it's still heartrending to read about. But, of course, what did I expect? What did *anyone* expect? A child whose mother he took from him! For Burroughs to be a loving father? Or ever to say to his child that he loved him? Still, it's somewhat unforgivable. It's frightening.

'Why?' I asked Bill. 'Why did you do this to all of us? And particularly, why did you do this to your son?' It was the most painful interview I've ever had. And very painful for him. He was kind about it – and time and a lot of blood had obviously gone under the bridge by then. Obviously he couldn't tell me what had happened, but he was very, very nervous. When I finally got to know him, the thing I always found strange was the fact that he was incredibly sensitive and incredibly needy. And you only find that out from his letters. You expected this very cold person. He may have been horrible to his son, but as a person, he was very fragile. In a way, it's almost as if he didn't want to break down in front of his son. Is that not possible? Because it's your son and because you love him, you're terrified of showing any emotion at all? My father was very like that. It's easy to say that in Bill's case it was drugs, but then look at Gregory.

The other great revelation I had at Naropa was getting to know Harry Smith, the great musical archivist and mystical filmmaker. He was a perceptive scholar of the odd, a Beat shaman, and an absolute sweet pea. He could be grumpy – oh, my, he was grumpy! Famously grumpy. But again, he was well worth it. I learned a lot from him. I already knew the Harry Smith *Anthology of American Folk Music* which generations of folkies – and especially Dylan – have mined for ancient Appalachian weirdness, but I didn't know his films and *that* was an eye-opening experience, all that use of painting things on to celluloid – that all came from Harry Smith. Harry was a true magus, he was the real deal. He was in that weird group, the Fellowship of the Golden Dawn. Aleister Crowley and Yeats had been members.

Harry didn't really give lectures, he just showed his films. He didn't talk much, either; he wasn't like Allen, he was the opposite of Allen and Gregory. They were both *huge* talkers. The word for Harry I think is 'hermetic'. Whatever he knew, he dispersed through his music archives and his films. He wasn't into making pronouncements. Harry, although terribly grand on one level, dwelling in the mystic realms, as a person was very modest, really; he didn't make a big deal out of things, he just got on with it. Life for Harry was going to the supermarket, cooking. He was dignified, and equally as nutty as the other Beats. He had a fetish about setting off fire alarms. If you're with him in those situations you have to say, I've never seen him before in my life! He's not with me!

What I found truly tragic was Peter Orlovsky's doomed place in the Beat hierarchy. His love for Allen mixed with his sexual confusion had put him in an impossible situation. By the time I knew Peter, he was totally alcoholic and desperate, and it was obvious that he wasn't really gay. He wanted someone to take care of him, he wanted to not be like his family, and he went along with being Allen's lover. He wanted to find a woman and have a family. Let's call it 'bi'. But, obviously, Allen couldn't bear that. It's better if he's an alcoholic and dying than bisexual! There's a very ruthless side to the Beats – they're much easier to deal with dead and on the page.

Despite all the problems and disillusionments at Naropa we were all secretly ecstatic to be there. Deb, as usual, put it succinctly:

I can't believe where I am and what I am doing. I am at the Jack Kerouac School of Disembodied Poetics and I love Allen Ginsberg and all his many character defects.

Allen, it's true, had tons and tons of flaws. But he also had this incredibly saintly vibe to him. Yes, he was a hustler and wanted to fuck everything in sight. But Allen also wanted to reach higher levels of consciousness, to be a good man. There was a huge paradox there, as we know; he wanted to fuck children, but he also wanted to be a saint. He worked terribly hard to get to bodhisattva level – I'm *not* trying to get to bodhisattva level, I'm happy if I can just be a decent human being – and it hasn't been all that easy.

One of the most touching things about Allen was what he did for Peter Orlovsky when Peter descended into terminal alcoholism – it was very tragic, and Allen loved him very much. Allen had seen what an effect Hazelden had on weaning me off my addiction and he probably thought this might work for Peter. At one point Peter said to Allen, 'I can't bear this; it would be better for me and for you if I just killed myself. That's what I'm going to do!' At which point Allen put him into Hazelden.

At Hazelden, as at all treatment centres, they now have what's called a Family Program; it's like going to an Al Anon meeting, but much more intense. You go if you're the brother, the sister, the mother, the father, the lover, the children, and join this family group. You're all strangers to each other, and you go and spend time with them every day, and a lot of shit comes out. I've never actually gone through that myself, but I hear it's extreme.

And Allen was prepared to do that because he loved Peter. It's an enormous sacrifice – especially if you're as famous as Allen was – and a profound way of showing your love for somebody, even if you have to go and out of you come toads and frogs' horns and nails and scorpions! I've no idea what they talked about, but I do remember that when Allen came back from that experience, he was transformed. He must have gone through his whole life with Peter up to then thinking that he'd done something terrible and that Peter's problems were his fault. The alcoholic may even encourage that. There's nobody more manipulative than an alcoholic. And they always manipulate the people closest to them the most. They know they can get away with it because the person loves them, so I'm sure Peter did a lot of that: 'I'd be okay if you weren't so successful' and all that shit. Oh, God, yeah.

Peter did stay off the alcohol, but he was very depressed. He never really got over it; he was doomed – doomed and lost. So, in a way, when the booze went, Allen lost his playmate, but that's how it goes, you know? Let's face it, the whole Beat way of life was a recipe for disaster.

Allen was always very fragile and delicate physically. Burroughs was ranting on and on about *yagé,* a psychotropic vine he'd discovered in the Amazonian rainforest and mushrooms and peyote and all those things, Allen, being Allen, and loving and worshipping Bill as much as he did, was up for it all. He wouldn't take heroin, and he wouldn't do cocaine, but if it was organic – mushrooms or something that came from the earth – he would try it even if it made him incredibly ill (he had a very delicate stomach). Old Uncle Bill had the constitution of a horse. We were never sure that he was entirely human.

Allen was always the most loved and the one with the biggest heart, but, actually, Gregory is the one, isn't he? They were all so outrageous, but Gregory went to the limit, extorting money out of that kid Sam Kashner for heroin – although, honestly, I don't think that's any big deal. Gregory was just like that. And you loved him or you didn't. He was well worth it. Whatever it cost the kid, it was worth it! He got a book out of it, didn't he – *When I Was Cool* – and a wonderfully funny, touching book it is. It's just that, as a parent, you send your kid to college, and then you hear that one of his professors is trying to fuck him and another professor is holding him hostage in a mountain cabin until he coughs up the money for the professor's angry fix. But, as Deb so aptly put it about Allen (and it could apply to them all): 'I'm so touched by Allen – I love him a little. He's not just an old Jewish fairy. He's not!'

Allen was a great example of somebody walking around with a big heart, and a big ego. He really wanted to be more famous than anybody, more famous than the Stones, more famous than Dylan, more famous than Bono. He wanted rose petals thrown and trumpets blown wherever he walked! You were tempted to remind him of that line from Milton's *Lycidas*: 'fame, that last infirmity of Noble mind'. I know that his shameless pursuit of fame was embarrassing, but when you love somebody, you don't care about their absurd vanities. And, in a way, it was kind of great. One of the hilarious things at Naropa was how all these Beatniks and Dharma bums – with the noble exception of Gregory – wanted to be rock stars and how they all wanted to get on stage with Dylan. They had an absolute obsession with Bob, even down to Peter Orlovsky's interrogation of Anne as to was Bob's arsehole clean?

Larry Fagin seemed a little intimidated by Allen, but, then, everybody was a little intimidated by Allen, except perhaps Burroughs and Anne Waldman. I certainly was, but Burroughs was very gentle with me. Very, very sweet. Naropa was Beats on the way down and there was something poignant about the whole thing. Sam Kashner describes it as Beats 'in a weird retirement home'. Billy Junior's description in Kashner's book is a little more jolting: 'They fell in front of a cracked mirror. And they fell in love with that cracked image. They'll just stare at it until they die.'

Gregory's bad conduct at Naropa was legendary. I heard all about his terrible behaviour from a friend of mine who worked at Naropa when Gregory was teaching there. She had two very beautiful daughters, one thirteen and one eleven, and she'd had a terrible time with Gregory running after her little girls at every opportunity. She coped, but she said it was an absolute nightmare.

He'd been chucked out of Naropa by the time I got there, but he was still being talked about. Allen, Bill Burroughs, they were all outrageous – but Gregory was just beyond belief. But just when he realises he's gone too far, he tells the kid Sam Kashner to go out and look at the stars.

It's a bloody shame that the faculty of Naropa threw him out, because he was a wonderful teacher in an extreme gangster-Zen way. When his wife left him, taking their baby, he completely *wrecked* one of the university apartments, and they threw him out.

Speaking of youth and its sorrows, there's a wonderful elegy for mad, raving Gregory at the end of Sam Kashner's book. Kashner's at the graduation ceremony – yes, they had graduation ceremonies and Parents' Weekends and all those things that other straight colleges had, and they finally did become an accredited institution of *higher* – in all senses of the word – learning. As Kashner graduates, he misses Gregory the mad monk:

> I thought of all the lunatics I had known at the Kerouac School and how I would miss them. And Gregory – where was he?
>
> Suddenly I could hear a howl from outside, like Quasimodo in the bell tower. It sounded like someone was yelling, 'Penguin dust!' It reached us in the shrine room while Allen was finishing his poem. It was Gregory's voice, shouting from outside the shrine room: 'Herald of the Autochthonic Spirit! That's it! Tell Sam Kashner – that's the title of our book!'

the curse of hollow tinsel bohemia

What the hell happened to bohemia? It took a hundred years
for Symbolist poets, absinthe-soaked painters, and talented
layabouts to create, and just twenty years for slick pseudo
hipsters to fuck it all up and dilute it into the latest designer
jeans ad. It's the curse of hollow tinsel bohemia! All that's
phoney rises, everybody's cool and nobody knows what the hell
it means. It's just prêt-à-porter bohemia. Consumer cool. Take
me back to the fifties! People say that's what the sixties were:
mass bohemia. Overnight everybody wanted to be a bohemian,
but I would have been happier back in the fifties with Gregory
Corso and Allen Ginsberg and William Burroughs, loving
Lenny Bruce and Jackson Pollock. Just imagine being able to go
and see Coltrane and Dizzy and Bird! The last of the giants,
and all that stuff. The fifties may have been, as some people
have said, like living in Soviet Russia, but it did produce some
great art and the wildest, most sublime jazz of all time.

I understand Bob Dylan's ambivalence about the sixties because
I share it. You may say it's perverse of me; well, I *am* perverse.
Art was more intense, purer in the fifties before the

flim-flammery of post-modernism. Sex was hotter, too – more repressed! And there was a genuine intellectual bohemia instead of the stoned mass bohemia of the sixties or this hipster-lite culture we have today. I would have preferred the fifties. I could have avoided a lot of trouble hanging out with the Beats, the Abstract-Expressionists. That bohemia was much smaller, much more authentic. The artistic community, even in the sixties, was very small. 'The Sixties' was actually very few people. In the sixties you could go up to the Stones' Maddox Street office and tell Mick some crazy idea you had and he'd listen to you – not that he'd probably do much about it, or Paul at Wimpole Street, but today it would be beyond belief what you'd have to do – apart from the fact that you wouldn't want to! There'd be fourteen lawyers prancing, seven accountants simpering, managers mulling, minders, minions, middle-men, media mentors, marketeers. Quickly, Allen, dear Auntie Allen, I need a time machine to take me back to the time when there were

> angelheaded hipsters burning for the ancient heavenly
> connection to the starry dynamo in the machinery of night . . .
> who bared their brains to Heaven under the El and saw
>   Mohammedan angels staggering on tenement roofs
>   illuminated . . .
>
> ALLEN GINSBERG, 'Howl'

caroline blackwood:
for all that i found there

Few people have defied reality, housekeeping, and common
sense with such relish (and hilarious results) as Lady Caroline
Blackwood. Her novels are dark fables and her life was just as
extravagant: heedless, magical, and filled with black humour.
I adored her.

It's hard to say which aspect of Caroline Blackwood is the more
fascinating: her hectic bohemian life or her gothic novels
steeped in irresistible malicious irony. Born into a wealthy
aristocratic Anglo-Irish family, she did everything to erase the
memory of her tormented, loveless childhood in a heedless,
headlong lunge into hedonism and a quest for the extreme. She
was very beautiful and rich, but what really held her friends,
husbands, and lovers under her mesmeric spell was her stinging
wit and nihilistic take on life. As a teller of grim tales she was
hilarious in her bleak, unsparing and remorseless view of
human character. Caroline had an almost medieval relish for
gargoyles – *Great Granny Webster* is a fantastically mordant
depiction of a life-stifling matriarch, and *The Last of the Duchess*

a wonderfully creepy double portrait of twin monsters in a necrophiliac relationship.

I've got to tell you the whole story of her wonderful last days – it was like a death scene from an improbable opera, complete with a large cast of children, friends, fellow writers, painters, musicians and ex-lovers crowding around her bed as if her whole life were coming to pay its respects. Even the weather cooperated in providing the appropriate setting: outside the wind was blowing snow against the windows – nature herself, as it were, bewailing the end of a great and wayward soul; which she was.

Caroline was staying at the Mayfair Hotel, which, if you're interested, is where the rich go to die. At the time I was appearing in Steve Paul's *Twentieth Century Pop* in the Rainbow Room at the top of the Rockefeller Center. It was a pop confection put together by Steve Paul with Darlene Love and Merry Clayton and me. We each sang songs separately as well as together. Darlene did a wonderful version of 'A Change Is Gonna Come', Merry Clayton sang 'Gimme Shelter' – as she had done on the Stones album *Let It Bleed* – and I sang 'Smoke Gets in Your Eyes'. It was a really rather wonderful thing, but very light. Keith came to see it – he came backstage and he was really sweet.

Caroline was a dear friend – more than that, an inspiration, a mentor, and a role model of the oddest sort, and I knew I had to go and see her but, as usual, not knowing what to do (I never do), I hesitated. On top of which it was physically very difficult to *get* to the Mayfair – outside it was an absolute, fucking blizzard, you couldn't see two feet in front of your face. The wind howled, the snow swirled down the street like a white devil. Marianne, I said to myself, just take a deep breath and go.

I'm such a twit in some ways. I dithered, I pondered, I procrastinated – my natural state – but not for too long because I knew I didn't have a lot of time. Our relationship had been music – not only music but the music of language. Not to mention a certain acerbic POV we shared. She'd written 'She's Got a Problem' for me – a devastating portrait of my self-destroying, errant self, and of Caroline's, too, of course.

I went several times – not out of obligation or even morbid curiosity but because she was such a hoot! The snow was so intense there was no point in taking a taxi, so I'd wrap up very, very warmly, and go through Central Park, *battling* my way across town, walking from the West Side over to the Mayfair. I would set out at about three o'clock and I'd get there about four-thirty. I found Caroline always on top wicked form. She wasn't going to let something like imminent death get in the way of a good time.

There would be Caroline, holding court, with her morphine pump (for her cancer), bottles of champagne and a tin of pâté, surrounded by her beloveds: her family, her daughters, except, of course, Natalya who by that time was dead. Caroline knew she didn't have long, but there was nothing morbid or self-pitying about her – far from it, the dire situation seemed only to pique her mordant sense of humour and taste for the absurd. Caroline dying in the Mayfair in wintertime in grand style. Oh, man, that was one of my best nights! I thoroughly enjoyed every minute of it, and the whole grand, giddy performance has gone down in Lowell family history (and several others, I imagine) as one of the maddest moments that anybody ever had on their deathbed.

I sat on the edge of her bed expectantly because she was such a connoisseur of human foibles and absolutely the best raconteur you could imagine. Caroline took a sip of champagne and told me a story. Because she knew she was dying, she'd been getting together with old friends that she hadn't seen for years and years and years – all rather grand, I gathered, you know, no names were mentioned – and, in the course of these reunions, she met up with this wonderful old friend of hers who happened to be in an equally bad way. We'll have to call her the Other Old Lady, like a character in a Pinter play. This old friend of hers also had cancer – and had also been given a morphine pump to handle the pain. They both had travelling morphine pumps so they could medicate themselves. During the reunion, overcome with affection and bittersweet memories, they fell into each other's arms, hugging and embracing and so delighted to see each other after all these years.

The excitement of seeing her old friend had exhausted Caroline and she began to feel the need of a little boost, so she hit her pump for a drip of morphine – but nothing happened.

'So I thought, fuck!' said Caroline, sitting up in bed for the denouement of her droll tale. 'What's the matter with this stupid fucking pump!' (This is how she was, you know, everything was 'Shit! Fuck! Cunt!') 'Fucking hell! I thought, the damn thing's not working. So I waited a bit, a few minutes – not *very* long, of course – and hit it again. And still nothing happened. But by now, as you can imagine, I was getting seriously pissed off. Meanwhile, the Other Old Lady was beginning to look quite sparkly – she was positively beaming, which irked me no end because I was feeling nothing, and so in an absolute fury I hit it again really hard and the other woman passed out. Somehow our morphine pumps had become entangled! The Old Lady fell down, completely whacked out by the loads of morphine I'd been pumping into her. Being hard core, I was used to much more morphine than this woman and almost ended up giving her a fatal overdose. A fine old reunion that would've been.'

Caroline laughed so hard at her own story she began choking. It was one of those pieces of black humour she so treasured. The absurdity, and even – or *especially* – the monstrosity of ordinary life were mother's milk to her. I loved the glee with which she viewed folly, wickedness and perversity. I've been horribly interested in her writing since I read her first book, a book of short stories, *For All That I Found There*. The title is taken from that wonderful Irish song, 'The Mountains of Mourne'. It was a tragedy she died so very young, she was such an impeccable recorder of the odd and outrageous – hellish stories in the manner of a Grimm fairy tale and told with the same innocent matter-of-factness.

The Stepdaughter is a very wrenching story about the gradual destruction of Renata, a fat, sluggish, disagreeable teenage girl. Whether it was intended as a portrait of her daughter Natalya, or not, Natalya took some of the descriptions of Renata very personally. Natalya took an even more morbid course in life than her mother – she became a junkie and died in the bath, having been shot up by Charlie T., who, when Natalya OD'd, climbed out of the bathroom window, took off, just left her to die in the bath. Well, that's so typical of junkie behaviour. Junkies do such terrible things. If he'd ever got clean, it's one of the things Charlie would've felt terrible about. Anyway, nobody else was there so nobody really knows what happened, and they're both gone. Natalya was found dead in the bath, blue, with a needle in her arm and Charlie later died of AIDS.

Natalya was the oldest of Caroline's four children (three daughters from her marriage to the composer Israel Citkowitz, and a son from her marriage to Robert Lowell) and suffered the worst from her mother's careless parenting. Caroline's children were the victims of her wilful life; they all felt rejected by her, Natalya being affected the most. She drifted into heroin addiction and an early death. It was in a way a reprise of Caroline's own loveless childhood, in which she and her brothers and sisters were brought up by servants in Clandeboye, the family's draughty great house in Northern Ireland. Caroline's feelings of abandonment and neglect are reflected in her description of the monstrous patriarch in *Great Granny Webster*, an ogress who presides over three generations of descendants. 'None of them could have the slightest importance to her, any more than all the leaves that have flown yearly from its branches can have much importance to an aged oak.'

Caroline had a great love of monsters, gargoyles, and dragonesses. One of her greatest creations is in a book of non-fiction, *The Last of the Duchess,* about the Duchess of Windsor and the ghoulish lawyer who kept her imprisoned, Maître Suzanne Blum. Because she couldn't get anywhere *near* the fucking Duchess, her book is about this macabre love affair/ sadistic captivity between Blum and the Duchess. I think that Caroline's theory was actually spot on, that the Duchess of Windsor was, by that point, in some kind of vegetable state following botched plastic surgery. Nobody was allowed to see her, she was comatose, almost dead, and was being kept alive *just,* but not allowed to die for a series of reasons ranging from greed to the unthinkable.

A master of concision and a devotee of malice, she communicates Blum's sinister gaze with a single sentence: 'Her slanting, unblinking eyes had a snakelike malevolence.' Caroline had brilliant instincts for things like that, and I'm sure she hit the nail on the head about a woman who really was *une monstre* – and, of course, it's so apropos, seeing that the Duchess was a bit of a monster herself, that she ended up in chains, shackled by this ghoul – who was obviously in love with her, too. That's the other shocking thing that I got from it, that there is the Duchess lying in bed, completely helpless in a coma, and the horrible *avocat* is having lesbian sex with her! And we *love* that idea. It's so grotesque, you know it's got to be true. It was now Blum who was the dominant partner, not only in their relationship as servant and master, but as lover, too. Caroline then takes the macabre union of the undead Duchess and her predatory *avocat* one step further than you could have imagined by implying that in some vampirish way Blum is actually sucking out the Duchess's life force and using it in some supernatural way.

People often described Caroline as a sorceress or a magician and she had come from a long line of witches and changelings. Her father, the fourth Marquess of Dufferin and Ava, was, according to his mother, a changeling, the real Marquess having been stolen at birth by fairies. Her mother was Maureen Guinness, one of the three heiresses to the brewing fortune. 'All witches,' wrote John Huston, capable of transforming men into geniuses and then back into swine without anybody noticing what had happened.

Which in a sense she did. She seemed to have a magical effect on the men she loved and married – and they in turn became obsessed with her (erotically and, by the way, financially – she was very rich). And she cast terrible curses on them when they left. Her first husband, Lucian Freud, made a number of portraits of her. In *Girl in Bed* she is a bewitching child woman with a changeling's spectral eyes. There's a hint of the children in *The Turn of the Screw* in those eyes, a child who can enchant you, seduce you, even, but who would just as soon cast a spell that will turn you into a toad. When she left Lucian (on grounds of mental cruelty) he began painting the corpse-like nudes for which he is now famous. While with Freud she spent a lot of time with wickedly witty painter Francis Bacon, whose

mordant view of life and aphoristic way of speaking she
absorbed into her writing. Her third husband was the poet
Robert Lowell, who described their turbulent relationship as:
'I'm manic and Caroline's panic. We're like two eggs cracking.'
He inspired her to write and she inspired one of his greatest
books of poetry, *The Dolphin*. When Lowell finally escaped
from the doomed seven-year relationship, he died in the back of
a New York taxi holding one of Freud's portraits of Caroline on
his lap.

Oh, and the other thing I want to tell you about is my last visit
to her. I felt I had to do something to express my – how can I
say it? – *fealty* to her – she was that grand. She gave me so
much: time and energy and song and laughter – and a kind of
gothic magic, even in those few days when she was dying, let
alone the rest of her life. True, she had given me trouble and
problems, but she was clearly an instrument of the sacred god
of chaos. She was 'Mad, bad and dangerous to know' as Lady
Caroline Lamb said of Lord Byron. She lived in expensive squalor
and was, as they say, 'a problematic house guest', the terror of
hoteliers. An alarming subject of interviews who invited adoring
journalists into rooms strewn with bottles, blood, and dirty
underwear to talk about the divine nature of language and the
more profane aspects of love. In later life when the demons she
had toyed with came out to claim her, writers like Steven
Aronson were stunned by her alarming appearance: 'I'd get
gooseflesh sometimes, because she was so haunted.'

But all of that was much earlier and long forgotten when
I stood at the foot of her bed wondering what to sing to her.

I cast my mind very far to every song I had in my repertoire – I realised I couldn't do the song she wrote for me, it was too sad. And because every song, even when written for someone else, is a self-portrait, and in this case the words were almost too painfully true. 'She's Got a Problem' with those telling words which were true for me, but even truer for the unrepentant but self-confessing Caroline:

> When I take my last ride
> Down the big dipper slide,
> Will I care, will it matter
> If the world should say:
> 'She had a problem.'
>
> She had a problem.
> She had a problem.
>
> In the end will it matter that you've gone?
> In the end will I go on minding that you've gone?
> Will the night always seem so long,
> Is it really darkest before dawn?
> Will I see whisky as a Mother
> In the end?

So, instead, I sang the Kurt Weill/Bertolt Brecht song 'Surabaya Johnny' for her a cappella. Can you imagine?

> I had just turned sixteen that season
> When you came up from Burma to stay
> And you told me I ought to travel with you,

You were sure it would be okay
When I asked how you earned your living
I can still hear what you said to me:
You had some kind of job with the railway,
and had nothing to do with the sea.

You said a lot, Johnny,
All one big lie, Johnny.
You cheated me blind, Johnny,
From the minute we met.
I hate you so, Johnny
When you stand there grinning, Johnny
Take that damn pipe out of your mouth, you rat!

When I finished singing Caroline and everybody else for a moment stopped the incessant chatter that went on day and night there – it was completely quiet. I was privileged to be at the court of a great sorceress.

I realised 'Surabaya Johnny' with its wicked, ambivalent lyrics, its mock exoticism, its poignancy and glamour and decadence of pre-Second World War Berlin – and, especially, its biting love/hate conundrum of obsessive romance – was the perfect choice of a song to sing for Caroline.

Surabaya Johnny,
No one's meaner than you.
Surabaya Johnny,
My god, and I still love you so!
Surabaya Johnny,

Why'm I feeling so blue?
You have no heart, Johnny,
And I still love you so!

Never for a moment during her last days did she lose her wonderfully dark, macabre humour. Even on her deathbed she was capable of cutting any portentous religiosity with bracing ghoulish wit. The novelist and fanatical Catholic revisionist Anna Haycraft appeared at Caroline's bedside bringing some holy water from Lourdes in the hope that she might grant the wicked, wayward Caroline salvation at her final hour, but in her clumsy way spilled the vial on Caroline's nightgown.

'Fucking hell, woman,' Caroline said, 'I might have caught my death!' With almost cosmic irony she died on 14th February 1996. St Valentine's Day.

'how goes the enemy?'

My father Major Faithfull was a spy in MI6, the intelligence service. He was such a brilliant linguist he could speak European languages without any accent because of his extraordinary musical ear. *Any* European language. So he was very valuable in that respect. They would parachute him in behind enemy lines with whatever he needed for his mission: some cheese sandwiches and the right clothes so that he could blend in with the natives.

One of these trips took him to Yugoslavia, where my uncle, Alexander Sacher-Masoch, was fighting with Tito and the partisans. And it was there that Glynn met Uncle Alex.

When my father finished his missions he'd always make his way back to Vienna. And so Alexander said to him, 'When you get back to Vienna, *please* would you see if my parents and my sister are still alive and everything's okay and give them all my love. And here is the address.'

Glynn must have been a very good spy because he never got caught. He arrived in Vienna and went straight to the

Hungarian consulate, where my mother and grandparents were living in a room right at the top. They were given sanctuary there because my grandmother was Hungarian.

Glynn rang the doorbell and Eva opened the door. He delivered the message from Alex and, Eva being so good-looking and lively and my father being a handsome daring spy, they fell in love on the spot. And from then on Eva became his connection in Vienna. How they would get messages back and forth I don't know. Glynn would just turn up, dropped by parachute somewhere – Germany, Czechoslovakia, Poland.

It's amazing he survived the war. He completed his missions brilliantly. It was harder for my mother; she had been a dancer in the Max Reinhardt company, led a glamorous life, and the war was one long round of privations and ongoing horrors. From Gitta Sereny's book, *Albert Speer: His Battle with Truth,* I realised what my father had been through. He had terrifying experiences. Sereny describes what it was like in Germany, Poland, Czechoslovakia, and I realised what horrors my father must have seen. The shallow graves at roadside Nazi executions with the hands and feet still waving as the dying writhed in a makeshift pit. It was only at the end of his life that he began to talk about these things and about his conversations with Himmler.

So my mother and father met under the most extreme and romantic circumstances imaginable. After the war my mother may have found peacetime difficult because in wartime she was a heroine and my father was a hero. They were in a very tense situation, taking great risks, and they both survived. At the end of the war Glynn came back deeply in love with Eva, and she with him. Except for one thing: she thought he was an English gentleman, a *normal* English gentleman. Little did she know how eccentric he was. And I mean that in the best possible sense.

Eva came to England and lived with Glynn while he was at Liverpool University doing his doctorate. His thesis was on Boccaccio and Petrarch.

He translated Michelangelo sonnets. He did little things like that, which is why he never rose very high in academic circles. He didn't write great tomes. He did what he loved and what amused him. But of course his big thing was Braziers Park – a sort of *quattrocento* commune devoted to great literature, great thinkers and utopian ideals, where my father taught for a number of years. Its ultimate goal was saving the world from its own destructive impulses. For my father the common culture of Europe – its artists, painters and philosophers – was at the centre of that.

As noble as all this was, my mother wasn't interested in saving the world – she had only by the skin of her teeth survived the virtual destruction of Europe. The war had taken its toll on her. She wanted to live a nice, quiet, normal bourgeois life – and that wasn't Braziers. Braziers was a bit of a mad house, to put it mildly, a nutty commune, and after a number of years Eva had had enough and she got out.

———————————

For most of his life, and, of course, throughout my entire childhood, my father had not been a particularly warm person. Like many people with ambitions to change the world, his passions were intellectual and conceptual. Glynn was the archetypal rational thinker – the thinker of great thoughts, in the classic European mode. His way of seeing the world basically came out of the Enlightenment – the idea that things could be worked out reasonably if one only examined them in a logical manner. This was obviously his reaction to the chaos and horror of WWII.

But following his illness, during the last two years of his life, an extraordinary change came over him. At some point he stopped eating and drinking and was obviously slipping away, and his family – my stepmother Margaret and my stepsister and brothers – panicked. They didn't want him to die, naturally, and took him to hospital, but there was a period there when he didn't have any oxygen and it affected the part of his brain that deals with emotions. Due to a decay in the synapses, my father's moods shifted radically from the controlled, stiff-upper-lip Englishman he had been, to a sentimental man unable to keep his feelings under control.

His reserve broke down and overnight he became emotionally volatile. It was a terrible shock – he had become touchingly vulnerable and susceptible to overwhelming emotional states. Long-lost people and incidents flooded him with poignant memories. He told me he deeply cared about the people in his life, had *always* cared about us, but had hidden it. It was then that I realised that he had always really loved me. He would burst into tears when he saw me, crying out distressingly, 'Oh my lost child, my lost child!'

As a result of his *crise* another strange thing happened to him. He found himself in a peculiar time warp; he couldn't remember anything after 1957. For a short while he was unable to recognise his wife or their children from his second marriage. 'Who are these people?' he whispered to me as I sat next to him. 'I have no idea,' I said. It's the worst thing I've ever done in my life, but I had felt left out all those years, felt they had usurped me in my father's affections. He'd ask, 'Where's Eva?' My mother had died several years earlier. But for some reason it never occurred to him to ask me, 'Why are you grown up?'

I was very lucky I got those last two years with him. I never would have known so many of the feelings he'd bottled up inside; perhaps even he was not in touch with that side of himself until after his illness. The letter he wrote to me after the book came out was so moving. It was from Braziers Park – on the letterhead there's a little engraving of a Gothic window.

Dearest Marianne, it began,

Just wanted to write to thank you for the copy of your book, which reached me today. It makes very interesting reading for anyone, but especially for me, of course. I think you've made a good job of it. I only now realised how difficult your life has been. I didn't know and I'm sorry, darling. You were a wartime baby and what happened to your mother and me we couldn't control. It was a strange wartime marriage of two rather difficult people that produced you, darling, and I feel proud, not only of your achievement in making a successful career, but of your success in growing into such a nice and mature person.

Lots of love,
Your Dad

That was a big moment for me. I really needed that letter. He hadn't known – and it must have been something he learnt from the book – how hard my life had been with my mother. He had no idea about what went on in that house: Eva drinking upstairs in her bedroom and me drinking downstairs – and no communication between us. On her part it was just uncontrollable fury, on mine, fatal resignation. Two lost souls shuffling about the house in a fog of rage and desperation. He could see it very clearly and it distressed him. After that we started to talk more.

His memory from the late fifties on may have been dim, but *before* 1957 my father's memory remained sharp. My father didn't have a lot of money but my mother always thought he had loads of dosh stashed away somewhere. He had always been very parsimonious. In his last years when I came to see him he'd splurge like mad because he knew how I always moaned and whined about the food at Braziers. He would take me to wonderful lunches and pay for them. During one of them we were sitting outside a glorious country pub in Oxfordshire. I might have had a gin and tonic, which is something I can't do any more. He turned to me under this beautiful apple tree in early June and began telling me stories from the war, about being dropped behind enemy lines, how his talent for languages allowed him to infiltrate. After the war the Russians, French, Americans, and English divided up the Nazi war criminals in preparation for their prosecutions at the Nuremberg Trials. Glynn came back when I was born and went out again as part of the crack team that was debriefing Himmler, the second in command to Hitler in Nazi Germany, and a true monster. As the chief engineer of the Holocaust, he had established the death camps, headed the Gestapo, and created the SS as the chief instrument of state terror. A major wasn't very grand but my father was the only one who could debrief Himmler. He was a clever psychologist, extremely personable and very English.

Himmler had been at the Wannsee Conference when Hitler clearly laid out the Final Solution. Speer's whole defence was he *wasn't* there and for that he didn't swing, though he got twenty-five years in Spandau Prison.

'He was a thoroughly unpleasant piece of work,' my father told me. 'A rat-faced little sadist who hideously lived up to his name.' (Himmler means 'heaven sender'.) 'Himmler relished grisly details such as the death's-head badges and daggers of the SS, and he's the one who came up with that revoltingly smarmy euphemism – *Sonderbehandlung,* "special treatment" – he used for the gassing of Jews, gypsies, homosexuals and other people he considered racially inferior.' But Glynn told me he also found Himmler an anomaly. 'Unlike the other freaks and twisted personalities in Hitler's high command, he seemed to be an ordinary, bourgeois man from a happy family. A happy

'I am erratic, neurotic, demanding, devious and fickle,' she wrote of herself – but so typical of Hen to omit her noble attributes: caring, clever, loyal, loving, witty, enthusiastic to a fault. Henrietta Moraes caught – how could it be otherwise – mid-thought, mid-sentence, mid-afternoon.

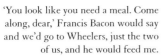

'You look like you need a meal. Come along, dear,' Francis Bacon would say and we'd go to Wheelers, just the two of us, and he would feed me.

With their impeccable manners and Elizabeth Arden make-up, the Jungman sisters, Teresa and Zita, were the last of their kind. Photographed, appropriately enough, by Cecil Beaton.

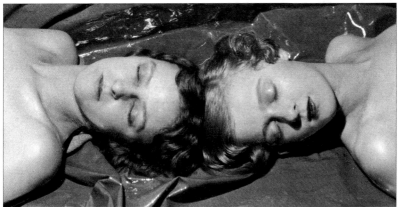

ABOVE Black pepper, red wine (for inspiration) and two Beat masters:
Allen Ginsberg and Gregory Corso.
BELOW 'So, see, man, a diminished seventh is kinda like Rimbaud in Abyssinia, dig?'
Dylan teaches Allen Ginsberg the abracadabra of guitar chords.

BRAZIERS ADULT COLLEGE

(BRAZIERS PARK SCHOOL OF INTEGRATIVE SOCIAL RESEARCH)

IPSDEN, WALLINGFORD, OXON OX10 6AN

0491 680221 & 680481

Jean Robertson, Chairman
Margaret Faithfull, Secretary

STATION: GORING (WR)

A. Maurice Roth BSc, Treasurer
Glynn Faithfull BA PhD,
Convenor of Studies

3rd Aug 94

Dearest Marianne

Just a note to thank you for the copy of your book which reached me today. It makes very interesting reading for anyone, but especially for me of course. I think you've made a good job of it. It was a strange war-time marriage of two rather difficult people that produced you, darling, and I feel proud, not only of your achievement in making a successful career, but of your success in growing into such a nice and mature person.

Lots of love

Your Dad

The letter my father wrote to me after my book came out touched me deeply.
Letterhead from Braziers Park, where my father taught for most of his life.

Pulling a song out of the existential darkness with cigarettes and lyrical regrets. Me and the noirish Nick Cave working on *Before the Poison*.

At the Berlin Film Festival with Patrice Chéreau where *Intimacy* won best picture (Golden Bear Award) in 2006.

Working on songs for *Before the Poison* with P. J. Harvey at my flat in Paris, 2004. That's me in the mirror thinking lyrical thoughts.

Jarvis wrote brilliant spiky lines for 'Sliding through Life on Charm' on my *Kissin' Time* CD. He *is* sort of like his lyrics in a way: whimsical, funny, quirky, wry. Me singing with Jarvis Cocker on keyboards at Festival Hall during the *Kissin' Time* Tour.

Banana, beer, and Barry. With his wicked wit, Barry Reynolds, my lead guitar player and soul mate, can always break the dreary spell of the road.

When my dear friend Perry Henzell, director of *The Harder They Come*, died last year I realised what a heartbreak it is to lose your soulmate. Perry and Sally Henzell at their home in Itopia, Jamaica, November 2000.

My grandfather, Arthur Sacher Masoch.

ABOVE Me in full sail at the Pigalle, 2007, with the inimitable Barry Reynolds at the helm.
BELOW At the 2006 Cannes Film Festival with cast and crew from *Marie Antoinette*:
Jason Schwartzman, Kirsten Dunst, Sofia Coppola, Thomas Mars, Steve Coogan, moi,
Ross Katz, and Aurore Clément.

family man who became a mass murderer!' For Glynn, Himmler seemed to embody the enigma of the 'good German', the average German citizen who under the influence of nationalistic rhetoric committed bestial crimes in the name of some abstract ideal. 'What you find with most bullies and sadists,' he said, 'is basically they're cowards. When Himmler saw his cherished wish of succeeding Hitler slipping away, he began secret talks with the Allies about Germany's surrender or turning Germany into an ally of the Western Allies against the Soviet Union. Hitler found him out and ordered his arrest. The British caught him as he was escaping.'

My father was beginning to unravel his twisted motives when Himmler killed himself – he'd concealed a poison capsule in one of his teeth. Remembering the incident, my father sat up in a rage and shouted, 'Bugger took the cyanide!' Unlike the Russian interrogators, Glynn had failed to search Himmler thoroughly enough – he'd missed the cyanide capsule and this false step had a disastrous effect on his career in MI6. If he had got Himmler to the Nuremberg Trials in one piece he would've been Sir Glynn Faithfull, everything would have been different.

I think the war had an exhilarating effect on a lot of people – it created a heightened reality. The sense of being under perpetual threat of annihilation made it a thrilling time to be alive. Under its heady atmosphere all kinds of unsuitable people came together – couples who, in peacetime, might not have given each other a second look. In many cases, the war brought people together who would *never* have met – as was the case with my parents.

The war, for all its horrors, broke down a lot of social and international barriers, and I think my father saw it as his mission to make that collapse of castes, nationalities and personalities into something positive. There were many who saw only devastation and horror in the war, but Glynn looked on it as a chance to begin again, to use the break-up to rebuild a new Europe out of the fragments. He thought it could be a new beginning for humanity in general, and, in a funny way, it has kind of worked out that way – for Europe, anyway.

When my father died I was in Vienna making a live recording of *The Seven Deadly Sins*. My father loved my early records, my folk songs – he was terribly proud of me, but I don't think he understood my *Broken English* phase at all. The title song with its refrain, 'What are we fighting for?' would seem to be almost emblematic of his mission – the fundamental inspiration for Braziers – world peace, international cooperation – but Glynn wasn't attuned to that kind of expression, or that kind of music *at all,* and, in a way, he didn't care. I would always give him my records, but I suspect he never listened to them. He wasn't really interested; he was only interested in his own stuff. For somebody who didn't like ego in other people, he had quite a bit himself – as my mother was always very quick to point out.

While I was in Vienna, Nicholas called François and told him my father had died. But François didn't want to say anything to me, because he knew how terribly upset I would get. Nicholas insisted, 'You *have* to tell her. Funeral arrangements are being made and Marianne will be devastated if she isn't told.' When François eventually did tell me I went into the strangest state where for about three or four days in Vienna I regressed to being six years old. In my mind my grandfather was still alive. I was in a state of suspended time. I would take François out on long walks in the streets of Vienna – I didn't know quite who I was or where I was, but when the moment came for the record I was fine. We were recording in the most beautiful place, the Konzerthaus, with Dennis Russell Davies and the Vienna Radio Symphony Orchestra, and, of course, it was the most incredibly emotional experience. We had a doc on standby, who might, or might not, give me a shot of Valium at the last minute, depending . . . In the end I decided not to and I'm very glad I didn't, because, despite being in a lot of pain, I was clear and that record has become one of my favourite records.

After the performance was over I asked the trumpet player from the orchestra if he would record 'The Last Post' so that I could play it at my father's funeral. From Vienna I went straight back to Braziers to take part in the funeral. I brought the cassette with me so Major Faithfull went into the sod in Ipsden church cemetery with 'The Last Post' played on a boom box. It played so well in that old country churchyard, I can't tell you. Very moving.

Memories of my childhood came streaming back to me as I stood bidding my father goodbye in Ipsden churchyard. Until the age of seven I grew up at Braziers. Things were madder, wilder, more eccentric, more randy, in the early years – some of the things that went on there were quite peculiar.

Braziers is an adult college where well-intentioned men and women – and students from other countries – come to contemplate the great poets and writers and ponder on the fate of the world. They appeared to be studying Dante and the Destiny of Man and all that, but what they were also doing was fucking like rabbits – with what were technically the *wrong* people. I remember creeping along the battlements as a child, spying, looking in windows. Nobody knew I was there, and, of course, I wasn't allowed to be there, but I was too curious. I could get up on to the roof and go round the whole house, listening in to people's rooms, and what was going on in those rooms was people having sex. I didn't quite understand what that was, but it didn't sound like they were having fun, in fact, it sounded kind of scary. There was sex going on everywhere at Braziers. Not exactly an entirely happy and positive experience for a kid, I guess.

After my parents split up I moved away with my mother. I had my own house with my mother and my little boyfriends and girlfriends at school – so I had another kind of life, too, apart from Braziers, which I think was helpful. I don't think it would have been so easy for me if I'd been in the commune at Braziers *all the time*. It would have been much more difficult, especially as I got older and I got pretty and all that – it was hard enough as it was. My father looked after me very well, he was very careful to make sure that none of those randy students seduced or molested me.

One of the things that I remember about my childhood is what a great teacher my father was and how much I learnt from him. He was always teaching, whether he was doing a course or whether you were just going for a walk with him over the

downs – it was all a sort of endless learning curve. My
education, such as it is, must have come so much from him –
and my mother. Glynn taught many courses on Boccaccio,
Dante, Alexander Pope, Teilhard de Chardin, plus a wide range
of intellectual topics: the destiny of man, the art of living, the
nature of group interaction, utopian communities.

Braziers was not – as these little utopian societies are in so
many Iris Murdoch novels – a religious community, but my
father must have been a little bit religious, considering his
intense interest in Teilhard de Chardin, the French Jesuit priest.
He must have had some sort of spiritual life rather like I do,
without being actively involved in any established religion. The
visions of William Blake were his idea of transcendent thought.
He was attracted to seekers and mystics who were outside any
conformist idea of religion.

He loved Cole Porter, and going to the theatre and movies. He
gave me a video of Bertolucci's *1900*; I have it still. He loved
poetry, Shakespeare, Dante. I recently came across a translation
he'd made of Dante's *canzone*, *Amor che nella menta mi ragiona*:

> *Love, as he talks within my mind,*
> *About my lady fair,*
> *Tells many things of her to me*
> *That cause my thoughts to err . . .*
> *For flames of fire her beauties are,*
> *Lit by a tender soul*
> *Which shatters evil, or makes hearts*
> *By honest thinking whole.*

He must have particularly loved those last four lines, which combine his love of poetry with his wish to 'shatter evil through honest thinking'. He was encouraged, when he read in *Se Questo E Un Uomo* (*If This Is a Man*), Primo Levi's memoir of his survival at Auschwitz, that in the camp Levi forced himself to recall certain cantos from the *Inferno* to reaffirm his humanity. If he could recite these cantos he was still a civilised man and not an animal. In cantos XXXI to XXXIV, Dante had peered into the depths of the eighth circle of Hell, the *Malebolge,* and prefigured some of the horrors Levi was experiencing, where

> *Weeping itself there does not let them weep,*
> *And grief that finds a barrier in the eyes*
> *Turns itself inward to increase the anguish.*

And he asks why the very earth does not swallow him up, or God intervene:

> *Ah! unyielding earth, wherefore didst thou not open?*
> *When we had come unto the fourth day, Gaddo*
> *Threw himself down outstretched before my feet,*
> *Saying, 'My father, why dost thou not help me?'*

In one of the most moving and prescient passages that Levi recited, Glynn saw that Dante's own inability to articulate the horror he beheld mirrored Levi's own speechlessness in the face of the Holocaust:

ché non è impresa da pigliare a gabbo
discriver fondo a tutto l'universo,
né da lingua che chiami mamma o babbo.

Which can be roughly translated as 'When attempting to depict the bottom of the universe this was not the time to speak in jest. In the face of such horror the tongue can only babble Mamma! and Babbo!'

My father's love of writing was infectious. I'm thinking about the time when I was really little and would sit in and listen to his classes. I'd always go to hear what he was teaching when I was growing up. After I started working myself, I attended his courses less and less, obviously, but I still remember my favourite passages. I was just reading some Petrarch last night in one of the books he left me. Petrarch's love poems tilt his love for Laura into a mad, pantheistic state where lovers morph into trees which then speak only of *her*.

Parme d'udirla, udendo i rami e l'ore
e le frondi e gli augei lagnarsi, e l'aeque
mormorando fuggir per l'erba verde.
Raro un silenzio, un solitario orrore
d'ombrosa selva mai tanto mi piaeque;
se non che dal mio Sol troppo si perde.

[In branches and leaves soughing in the wind and in the complaints of birds I hear her, and in water murmuring as it flows through the green grass. Never has such silence, or the desolate terror of a dark wood so pleased me. The only thing is that I've misplaced the Sun which meanwhile has got lost somewhere.]

His love of learning and the discovery of the brilliant fact that illuminates the mind is so ingrained in me that when I hear something wonderful about one of his heroes I want to call him up and tell him. I forget that he's gone. Someone told me recently that *italic* in printing is based on Petrarch's handwriting.*

As steeped as Glynn was in the narcotic lyricism of the Renaissance, he was not a dry academic *at all*. He very much believed in love and sex as a vital part of life, as you can see from the things he liked and the mad stuff he encouraged at Braziers. My mother had nothing but disdain for the whole business. She just didn't understand it – she thought it was all completely fake. But I did kind of get it. I understand what my father was trying to do and I understand where it came from: it came out of his experiences in the war – he wanted to do something to help people communicate better, through intellectual discussion and through the transcendent visions of the great poets and writers, Shelley's 'unacknowledged legislators of the world'. The mixture of high utopian thoughts and randy sex might seem incongruous but it was very much of its time – the 1950s – and an uncanny harbinger of the heady free-love, let's-change-the-world vibe of the sixties. It was the fifties, the intellectual, Bertrand Russell-ish fifties, when Braziers began and there were all these ideas – grand,

---

* Professor Robert Glynn Faithfull would have particularly loved this.

world-mending ideas, small groups of people isolating themselves from the big bad world to study Big Ideas, ideas about the Nature of Man, the foundations of civilisation, the complexities of communicating ideas. Along with the metaphysical deliberations came experiments in group consciousness. This combo – shagging and Schopenhauer – was as rampant at Braziers as it is in the novels of Iris Murdoch. Murdoch has been accused, rather unfairly I think, of writing Harlequin romances for highbrow (a highbrow, as wittily defined by Brander Matthews, being 'a person educated beyond his intelligence'). She writes, it's been said, 'for people who can't take either their romance or their religion straight and who need the one to justify to themselves their indulgence in the other.' To which I say, 'Carry on!'

Glynn wanted people from different countries and backgrounds to interact together in whatever way they wished so the kind of situation which gave rise to WWII wouldn't happen again. That's why he had all these Italian, German, Swedish students coming: young people from all over Europe. He was entirely Eurocentric – his thinking didn't go beyond Europe. He thought (and I think he was right) that if people could see how each other lived, come together in a beautiful place like Braziers and talk, it would lead to a less messed-up world. It wasn't only about the intellect, not at all. His idea was to integrate the intellectual pursuits with communal living. Everybody had something to do in life, everybody had a role, a job. He was very practical in that way. One of the interesting things he said about communal living was 'if you ever run a commune' – something I am *never* likely to do – 'change people's jobs.' If one person's the cook this month, then the next month get someone else to be the cook. That way they don't become tyrannical about their area. This was a domestic extrapolation of a Braziers principle: to avoid the concentration of power in a few hands. He was interested in how the ego can twist and thwart everything. He was a philosopher of the group mind, almost a technician of group dynamics – how to deal with the ego within the group.

It's something I've applied to my own situation – had to be dragged kicking and screaming into, actually, in what *I* do – because my entire professional life has involved dealing with groups, rock groups – my own and other people's – and situations in the recording studio where you're dealing with a lot of different people and their egos (and mine). I'm about to make another record and I have to remind myself once again to leave my ego behind when I go into the studio. Your ego doesn't exactly help when you're working together on a project where everyone comes into the session with their exalted ideas of themselves, their hurt feelings, their need to be acknowledged by you.

Recently I came across a quaint memento from Braziers: written contributions from a series of three courses given there – one of them taught by my father. The courses were: 'Spring Freedom'; 'Aspects of Love'; 'Harvest reflections: Aspects of Death'. My father contributed his translation of a Dante *canzone* which I quoted above and my stepmother, Margaret, wrote this charming evocation of Edwardian paganism straight out of *The Golden Bough*:

SPRING IN BRAZIERS

Throw out the old. Bring in the new. A time of re-assessment
and appraisal. The dried flower arrangements, friends of
winter, go. Bring in a world of affluence, a house of gold
bursting with daffodils, primroses, narcissi, and then still
more. Old patched trousers do their last proud play, then
out for cleaning rags . . . The sun is poking his finger round
the door . . . The call, the challenge is there. Throw winter
apathy away. Sing in the new.

It's *so* Braziers! Braziers was so straight out of an Iris Murdoch
novel, it was as if she'd *written* the whole place – and she
almost did, actually. In 1958 – just eight years after Braziers
began – Iris wrote a novel about a commune called *The Bell*.
Which very well might have been based in part on Braziers. It's
about a lay community of well-intentioned seekers attached to
an abbey, and Braziers does have an abbey feel to it, it's all
Strawberry Hill gothic, very beautiful with poppy-lined paths
and moss-encrusted cottages.

My dad might well have met Iris Murdoch – they travelled in
the same circles, Iris taught philosophy at St Anne's College,
Oxford – which is only sixteen miles from Braziers, so she must
at least have heard of the place, a living embodiment of her
fictional worlds. Glynn and Iris certainly shared similar
obsessions. *The Bell,* like countless other Murdoch novels, is
concerned with the problem of how a group of troubled
seekers-after-transcendence try to live ethically in a corrupt
world despite their own flawed personalities.

Murdoch created fictional microcosms in which she studies her characters as if they were under a microscope. Braziers Park School of Integrative Social Research – to give it its daunting full title – was founded as a conscious and ongoing experiment in communal living. In other words, it is its own subject – a kind of novel, essentially, which observes itself in order to find out what's going to happen. Braziers' mission statement – 'To make conscious the shape of the process of which we are a part, so that we may facilitate its development more efficiently' – borders on tautology *and* unintentional humour. As a character in *The Bell* says, 'trying to live up to ideals does often make one look ridiculous'.

One of my father's more whimsical mannerisms was to look up at the clock and say, 'How goes the enemy?' meaning time, or perhaps we should say Time, with a capital T. The phrase comes from an obscure eighteenth-century play called *The Dramatist* by Frederick Reynolds. The line is spoken by a character named Ennui the Timekiller, 'whose business in life is to murder the hour'. It was a catchphrase – generally spoken somewhat wryly – of my father's generation, but my father I think took it a bit more earnestly. I wish I could say that from Glynn I learned the valuable lesson of never wasting time, but wasting time happens to be something I'm very good at. My particular interpretation of the old adage would be: If you *are* going to idle away your time in *dolce far niente*, at least do it gracefully.

fuck off, darling!
(my beloved henrietta moraes)

Dear brave, wild, chaotic, heroically self-indulgent Hen! The
epitome of that wilful, inspired, prodigal bohemian life that's all
gone now. She was a writer, muse, model for Francis Bacon and
Lucian Freud, and the Queen of Bohemia in the dives of Soho
and the *haute hipoisie*, a wayward and radiant spirit whose
reckless intensity magnetically attracted people to her. Hen had
friends from the gutter to the aristocracy and on through the
grand literati whom she both terrorised and enchanted – Cyril
Connolly, Sir Mark Palmer, Philip Toynbee, Johnny Minton and
twenty-odd sailors.

She was a precocious little *Existentialista*, at an early age a
habitué of infamous Soho watering holes. Having oysters and
champagne with Francis Bacon at Wheelers on Compton Street,
hanging out with a very sharp crowd at the Gargoyle Club on
Meard's Street, a seedy drinking den and haunt for artists like
Francis and Lucian Freud, where the painter, and Hen's dear
friend, Johnny Minton danced his frenetic fandangos. Or the
Colony Room where Bacon, Freud, Michael Andrews and
Frank Auerbach – 'Muriel's Boys' – lurked in an environment

designed for those who thought of themselves as misfits, cunningly created by the autocratic and temperamental owner Muriel Belcher who was accustomed to greeting female patrons with a cheery, 'Hello, Cunty!'

Hen was one of the great beauties of the fifties, the favourite model of Lucian Freud and Francis Bacon – he painted her some eighteen times. She almost at once fell under his magnetic sway, as she said, 'like a mesmerised rabbit'.

Hideous Kinky – the film with Kate Winslet about a hippie chick with two little girls in Morocco – was based on a book by Lucian's daughter, Esther. In the book Lucian was the father of the little girls (in the movie they turned him into a writer). The Winslet character goes to Morocco to get away from Lucian – she can't take Lucian any more 'cause he's tough to live with – you pick that up from Henrietta's book; people are frightened of Lucian.

Then there were the notorious pornographic photos John Deakin shot of Hen for Francis Bacon. Francis had asked Deakin to take some pictures of her to be used as the basis of a painting. Deakin perversely took this as an order to shoot hundreds of close-up, wide-angle shots of her pussy, and Hen in other erotic poses. When Francis saw them he said, 'The blithering idiot has got the pose reversed,' and had Deakin shoot them all over again – these became the basis for two versions of *Lying Figure with Hypodermic Syringe*. He painted many 'studies' of her as well. I think what attracted Francis to Hen was her aura of danger and impulse – the actual writhing, breathing pulse of life itself — even in such desolate paintings of her as these. A few weeks after the first photo session with Deakin, Hen came across him in a Soho drinking club flogging them as dirty pictures to a bunch of sailors for ten bob a pop. Unfazed, she merely said, 'I don't really give a damn about your selling pictures of my cunt, John, but you could at least buy me a large drink. *Several* large drinks.'

Wonderful, wicked stories poured out of her and *about* her. Hen was blessed with a thirst for ecstasy and oblivion, a bold eye for a promising sexual encounter (disregarding sex or age), and uncanny antennae for alcohol or drugs. She inhabited a sort of enchanted space where the oddest, most unlikely things happened. She travelled on her own loopy groove, avoiding the straight world entirely. Her haunts were the gay underworld of Soho, mad painters, Hell's Angels types, the *jeunesse dorée*, mystics, antiquarians, Indian poets, and second-storey men. And most bizarrely of all, she took a secretarial class with that equally unlikely typing pool candidate, Caroline Blackwood, 'who looked like I felt . . . stockings falling down and bored by the mysterious shorthand'.

On and on went the irrepressible Hen. She became absorbed in avant-garde theatre. Drawn to morbid and pathological subjects, she wrote articles for *The Times* and *Oz,* and on LSD watched as 'Groovy Bob', Robert Fraser, sprouted horns and danced. In Paris she hung out with Allen Ginsberg and Gregory Corso. William Burroughs greeted her with, 'Good day. I hate women. Women are like birds, they sit on the window sill and tap, tap, tap on the glass.' He then showed her his track marks.

She had a brief and disastrous career as a cat burglar and a somewhat longer career as a methedrine addict. When she shot liquid meth – a terrifying drug sometimes used to resuscitate the dead (and Hitler's favourite pick-me-up) – it made her as ecstatic as St Theresa: 'It lifted me up to a wave,' she wrote in her autobiography, 'and I coasted home at the speed of light on its crest: a duck to water.' 'I picked up bad habits like a magnet does iron filings,' she said of herself.

Amphetamine psychosis soon led to serious mental derangement which in turn led to an even more risky obsession: burglary. She used to shoot up loads of methedrine and go thieving in Hampstead with some geezer named Stan. At first it was just the thrill of it: shinning up drainpipes and climbing in windows to make off with bric-à-brac – towels, ashtrays and so on – but eventually it got a bit more serious. After doing some drinking, smoking a little hash and taking enough pills to light up Liverpool, she and her partner in crime broke into a neo-Georgian mansion on a fragrant May night. They leisurely partook of cocktails at the posh little bar in the living room – they considered themselves artists, so none of that rushing about shoving stuff into sacks business for them. They took off with Meissen china, a child's Stradivarius, and other pretty stuff. By the time they got out of there the sun had come up.

They would probably have got away, but couldn't resist just one more spot of petty larceny, this time for food. The shopkeeper ran after them, yelling, 'Stop thief!' Stan evaporated like snow in the sun and Hen found herself running down the High Street with a bag over her shoulder that might as well have been labelled 'swag', with candlesticks and teapots poking out of it. By now the shop owner, the milkman, newspaper delivery boy, Uncle Tom Cobley and all were chasing after her, yelling, 'Stop thief!' And as in a dream she felt her legs become more and more leaden. Unable to run, she was apprehended by a large George Formby-type copper who astutely observed, 'You don't know what time of day it is, do you, darlin'?' Or what year, he might just as easily have added. She ended up in Holloway Prison. They interrogated her for hours, but she refused to give up the name of her partner – she was incredibly cool and honourable. Eventually a kindly intellectual probation officer, realising she wasn't exactly a career criminal – of this sort, anyway – sprang her.

She was a helluva lot of fun and incredibly cultured. By the time I knew her she was no longer shooting meth, but once you're a speedfreak you never lose that speedfreak jive. She would just go off on many many subjects – she was psychic, saw big red cubes with the number fifteen inscribed on them, read the tarot, and, less supernaturally, perhaps, heard voices telling her, 'Henrietta, I think you should go to Ireland now.' She would tell these wonderful, hair-raising stories: Rebel, the South African rudeboy who lived in the number 18 bus at the Battersea depot and came into her life like a boy riding the Big Dipper, the ghoulish ghost of number 9 Apollo Place, with its breathing sofa, buckets of blood and a decapitated head. A few years ago I went to do a shoot in Apollo Place. The photographer told me that her old house was now a Narcotics Anonymous meeting place – Hen would have loved the irony.

I couldn't begin to tell half the Tales of Henrietta – and there are as many stories about her beloved dogs – dachshunds, brindled lurchers, sheepdogs – as there are about people. You'll just have to read her wonderful memoir, *Henrietta*. 'Mustn't Grumble' was the brilliant title Hen came up with for her book, but the dodos at Penguin wouldn't let her use it. They insisted on *Henrietta*. 'Mustn't grumble' is very much from the war and her parents, her mad mother. I'd use *Mustn't Grumble* for my own book, it's such a good title, except that it wouldn't work for me – I grumble *endlessly*. It represents a genuine kind of stoicism that I don't actually have. But it was *perfect* for Hen.

Hen was so endearing people would just adopt her out of the blue, take her in, give her houses, dogs, drugs . . . In the fifties she was the queen of Soho's artistic scene, in the sixties she became the mascot of hippie mystagogues in search of the ever elusive Holy Grail.

Hen, decked out in boots from Granny Takes a Trip and Antique Market shawls, took to the hippie trip like a fish to water, but then she took to practically *everything* like a fish to water: alcohol, methedrine, gardening, sex, cat burglary, writing, Arthurian questing . . .

Sir Mark Palmer – but let's just call him 'Mark' for fuck's sake! – spent the late sixties on a quest for the Holy Grail in the caravan with loads of exquisitely dressed people. 'Why don't we travel across the land like gypsies and be free?' Mark asked, and since nobody could see any reasonable (or unreasonable) objection (they were all as stoned as he), they bought a

barrel-top gypsy wagon and a brown and white horse they
dubbed Rizla, and off they went in search of the ineffable,
unfindable, once-and-future whatnot. A whimsical itinerary:
Camelot, Glastonbury Tor, Tintagel (where Arthur, it's said,
was conceived), Boscastle (where Merlin lived), Launceston
(supposedly Sir Lancelot's town – although better known for its
steam railway – and flying saucers, of course). How they came
into a quest for the Holy Grail was . . . oh, never mind.

It was a motley crew. Some of them just came and went, like
Chrissie Shrimpton and John Dunbar, my ex-husband,
cutting-edge art dealer and scene-maker, dropping in, dropping
out – the moveable feast people. Then there were real
hard-cores who signed on for the *entire* quest. One of them was
Henrietta, and another was Penny Cuthbertson, who married
Desmond Guinness. A lot of people joined Mark's endless
children's parade: Nicholas Gormanston, Julian and Victoria
Lloyd, Michael and Jane Rainey, Christopher Sykes, Christopher
Gibbs, Catherine Tennant, and, as a sort of mystic dowser of
ancient ley lines, cosmo-archaeology, ranter against the metric
system, scholar of the temple of Jerusalem and explicator of
Christ, the Great Cock, John Michell. All sorts of people were
looking for the Holy Grail, but it was Mark's *mission*.

And it all went along with this very strict hippie rule book
about only eating macrobiotic food, avoiding anything edible
that was white (bread, sugar), not taking baths and not using
any medicine – which caused some very funny things to
happen, you know. If anyone got the clap or crabs they had to
suffer through it, which essentially meant they never got rid of

them. Despite their abhorrence of chemicals, they made exceptions, of course, for drugs like LSD. People would get *yelled at* for having a slice of processed cheese. And, Hen, of course, used to get into terrific trouble because of her drinking and general sort of drugging around and hell-raising – and occasionally burning down one of the caravans as a result of smoking in bed drunk.

Mark was very doctrinaire about all the lysergic pieties – the way acid heads sometimes get, funny thing, that – so Hen's Dionysian abandon would really *flip* him out. She was by no means the only one breaking the sacred code, but she was the one who would always get caught. And I would put myself in that category, too! Which is why I would never go on these caravans. Never did. I loved the *thought* of it, you know; loved the idea that there were loads of my friends going round England all the time in search of the Holy Grail.

I had the same reaction to communes. I grew up in a commune, for chrissake, having from an early age to talk to people who I didn't know – had to, because that was what my father insisted on – and I just didn't want to go there again. Communes and caravans brought back bad memories. I simply thought, I just can't do this! Well, I'm a Capricorn and it may be dopey astrological crap, but I think Capricorns need a lot of private time. Musicians being the exception. But for group activity, I have absolutely *no* aptitude – or interest. I wanted what I'd never had, which was a lovely house with my lover, my child, my friends, a kitchen, a bathroom, all those kinds of things.

Mark and his children's crusade weren't always on the road. Sometimes they would stay in some grand house for long periods of time – they parked their gypsy caravan at Mick's house, Stargroves, for months. It took them *four years* to get to Wales, for heaven's sake – so a lot of detours to investigate mounds and tors, and ley lines and Arthurian antiquariana. They were living in this quasi-medieval bubble that had nothing to do with the straight world – all the magical, mystical, lysergic lore of the sixties taken to extreme extremes.

Hen was a trusting, vulnerable soul and she got badly taken advantage of. Mark and Kelvin Webb bullied her into shaving her head and she ended up with this terrible shiny green knob – bad enough on a country road with a parade of freaks but utterly humiliating on the King's Road in the middle of the afternoon where the groundlings hooted at her and called her names.

But nothing really fazed Hen – she always ended up with feet on the ground or head above water. Once while travelling on a barge she got knocked off into the canal during a collision. She emerged covered in weeds but with the book and the joint she'd been smoking still in her hands.

———————————

All right, new scene: We're in the early seventies, and I'm back from the brink, I'm not living on the street any more, and I'm not shooting smack any more, so all that's happened, done and gone. I can't quite figure out the year – as you know, I'm always very hazy about the *exact* time frames, but it must be somewhere like '73 – and, as you probably recall yourself if you've lived that long, everything was changing in everybody's lives. Remember that? First of all we had to admit (sort of!) the sixties were over, pretty much, and we had to change a lot of our ways. And one of them was Mark Palmer and his caravan.

The Great Quest eventually had to come to an end, and at that point Mark wanted to, had to, *dump* a lot of people, because he was going to get married to Catherine Tennant. When the caravan halted, Henrietta was one of the most difficult cases, because she literally had nowhere else to go. So dear Mark decided that Hen should find out if I would take her, and I said, 'Well, all right then, yes, I will,' because I liked her very much and although she was in some ways a big problem – no question about that! – she was also great fun.

Hen was very well read, which you wouldn't immediately guess. She was older than me, so I didn't actually know her in Reading, but she'd gone to Queen Anne's School in Caversham just outside Reading – the girls wore very smart red cloaks and they were very posh indeed; much posher than Saint Joseph's where I went – or at least we always thought so – and, of course, it was Protestant. Her first crush was Valerie Fletcher, a girl at Queen Anne's who slept with a volume of T. S. Eliot's poems under her pillow and eventually married 'Tom' after he'd shunted his first wife, Viv, off to the loony bin. Hen was thus part of a very elite, intellectual milieu, and, astonishingly, dreamt in manuscript form. 'All my dreams,' she said, 'are *written* by me. I dream in sepia-coloured pages, flowing quill-penned lines in Aramaic . . .'

She was very erudite in many ways, which Mark Palmer, God bless him, is not. He's good-looking, very thin, all sorts of great qualities, but clever? No. Mark was always so much more interested in riding than reading, basically. He wanted to be a jockey and, in fact, did become a jockey for a little while when he settled down in the West – Byford Heath in Gloucestershire, I think it was called, in a lovely house where he kept horses and rode. He was always very conscious of appearances – how one looked aesthetically – things like never putting on weight mattered to him far more than any aphorism by Ludwig Wittgenstein. He was one of the beautiful people, and he *was* very beautiful – still is. Mark never let himself go, let's put it like that.

So that intellectual side of Henrietta I don't think Mark ever appreciated, but I certainly did, and so she landed on me. Talk about the parachute woman. Anyway, by this point I'm off the streets and living in a little mews flat which belonged to a friend of my mother's in Hanover Terrace. It wasn't particularly nice, but it was perfectly all right, and Hen *loved* it. It was in Regent's Park. You know the big Georgian houses off Regent's Park? Well, there were little mews flats at the back, and this particular one had a view of the park and of Queen Mary's rose garden. Henrietta came to live there with me. Obviously, I couldn't pay her anything, all I could do was offer her what I had, which was my little bit of nothing. At least I wasn't on the dole – I'd never been on the dole and I never wanted to.

'Life with Marianne, in a mews flat in St John's Wood,' she wrote in her book with exemplary tact, 'was fairly desultory to start with.'

There were two beds and a kitchen and a tiny sitting room and a bathroom and that was all. So Hen came and shared that. A lot of the time I was away. I would be going off to do some work on something, and Henrietta in the beginning must have been on her very best behaviour. I can't remember anybody really treating me as nicely as she did until François came along.

She would get up and make me breakfast and a cup of tea and bring it to me in bed. I was absolutely blown away. She had that fantastic sort of charming I'm-taking-care-of-you side, and I thought her arrival was a great, wonderful event. But, I mean, at the same time, she was always having these dreadfully unsuitable boyfriends. Really!

Rather charming blokes, but truly dodgy characters when it came down to it and things began disappearing from the flat. One day I went out and when I came back a Persian silk prayer rug, one of the most beautiful things I'd saved from Cheyne Walk where I lived with Mick, was missing. It fills me with horror to think what Henrietta and her lousy, thieving boyfriend got for this museum-level carpet – probably thirty bob, or at most thirty pounds.

But with Henrietta the pluses were always bigger than the minuses. I'm sorry I lost my beautiful Persian prayer rug, but

the living, breathing Henrietta was far more valuable to me, a
life-saver, actually. She'd been in the mouldy, mucky, ratty,
moley country looking for the Holy Grail for years, and
suddenly she's back in the good old Smoke, with somewhere to
live, food to eat. Well, for one thing, she got all our drugs
sorted. Through our hooker friend Michelle – my actual friends
at the time were these working girls in London – we got a
fabulous drug connection. She got some doctor completely
under her sway so that he was writing scripts for
amphetamines, black bombers, and Mandrax and all that stuff
as fast as we could fill them. We lived on Green Groovers –
that's speed and barbiturates mixed – which Henrietta
remembered very fondly in her book. As Hen describes it in her
quaint, Dickensian way:

> I used to go to him [the doctor] once a week to keep myself
> together and fell in with a group of ne'er-do-wells whom I
> met in the chemist's. We used to go 'brickering' together,
> browsing through skips and empty houses, finding all sorts
> of good things. 'Brickering' is a highly enjoyable sport when
> charged up on amphetamines.

I can imagine! It was great fun for a while, like one long
non-stop party, in fact, in this *tiny* little mews house, and then
at some point I started flagging and then it all became a bit
much for me. I started to think: 'I don't know if I can deal with
this!' I couldn't go on. And so one day I slyly, and not
completely disinterestedly, began thinking: 'Well, what would
you do if you were Henrietta and you were very firmly being
nudged out of the nest?' And I thought, well, what I would do

is get a job. That's the logical thing to do, you know, if you're living with somebody who has no money and there's no trust fund, no nothing, someone who can barely look after herself. There was one problem with this logical train of thought: it was the one notion that would never ever have occurred to Hen. I waited and waited for her to get a job, but Henrietta had not the slightest inclination to work for a living – none at all.

Well . . . we've all been in this situation a million times, and you know there comes a point even for talented layabouts where you say to yourself, 'Right, I've got to find something to do!' Write a book, make a record, sell drugs, you know, *something*. But if you haven't got an aptitude for any of these things, then you just get a job! I mean, I never said anything, but I always thought she'd be really happy as a barmaid, and very good at it, but she didn't want that – or anything remotely like it. There was something so sort of *twisted* about her attitude – not in a bad way – but, to be honest, her approach to work was practically *sociopathic*. She absolutely didn't want to be on the side of the normal straight people with jobs; she would have rather *killed* herself. As Hen herself would be the first to admit:

> I dropped out. I started to retreat. One morning I woke up and, instead of leaping into the bath and off to work, I lay in bed and thought, To hell with it, I've had enough. I'm just not going to spend my life dreaming up ways to sell pens and cars and sausages and beans. I stayed in bed for six weeks, watching television and drinking Teacher's whisky – I believe I liked the name.

It was hopeless, in other words, to wait for Hen to get a job, so while staying at Hay Castle I plotted to palm Hen off on to poor old Richard Booth, the guy who started the whole massive bookstore thing at Hay-on-Wye – what's now the Hay-on-Wye Festival and all that. At that time, he was just really starting, buying up *thousands* of books and opening these *huge* bookshops in Hay. I used to go and stay at Hay Castle with him. But I never had any romantic thing with Richard; I managed to keep him at arm's length, which I'm very good at doing.

Working for Richard wasn't exactly like a straight job – in fact it was quite mad; one of her co-workers was a defrocked ex-Bishop who had been caught in a dalliance with a chorus girl. Hen *tried* to do the Richard Booth thing, shelving tattered, musty, esoteric books as they came out of the packing crates at a frenetic rate, cataloguing them: D for Dickens, dowsing, Doolittle, Damocles, dilatory domiciles, the dodo and the Domesday Book. T for Thackeray, thatching, *Thumbnail Sketches of Tuscany*, Thucydides, and *Tennis for Teenagers*. That lasted for about six months, then Hen had had it. She began dreaming about books, books parading down the High Street, talking to her – given the number of pink gins and Watson's Ales she was consuming on the job, it's hardly surprising. Eventually Richard couldn't take her any more and, with the same exasperated tone that Henry II must've used about Thomas Becket, he confessed to me, 'I'd fire her except that I can't think of anyone in their right mind who would employ Henrietta.' As quick as two shakes of a lamb's tail, I said, '*I* will.'

Hen was one of those people who could exasperate you and drive you around the bend – you'd be utterly fed up with her, but six months later you really missed her and craved her company. I decided to see if it would fly if Henrietta looked after me. That was a very funny idea, yet another case of the blind leading the blind, so to speak. So we had a seriously good stash, and we availed ourselves of it freely and off we went on tour with it, and when we ran out, we found a doc in Ireland. 'Minding Marianne,' Hen wrote in her understated way, 'turned out to be all-consuming.' Hawk Records was the promoter of the Irish tour she came on, a ruthless, hard-nut bunch locally known as 'the Murphia'. *The tour took us all over Ireland*, she wrote,

> and sometimes involved hours and hours of driving, with stops at Little Chefs and hurried, greasy meals and snacks. I had never been on this sort of road and I found it absolutely exhausting, and the Murphia and I disliked each other with some passion . . . I liked gigs, though. I liked it when we actually arrived and were all set up and the gig started. Marianne is very popular in Ireland, everybody loves her. They think of her as a cross between a convent girl and a witch. When her small blonde figure appeared on stage, a roar of tumultuous applause would go up and we would be away.

First gig was at a big place called the Snake Pit. Standing in the wings, I looked out at the crowd through the curtains. I was absolutely petrified. I couldn't move. My knees froze, lockjaw set in. In a *tiny* voice I told Henrietta I couldn't go on and proceeded to throw up on her. I felt this was a pretty good

confirmation of my inability to perform that night, but Hen
wasn't having any of it. She spun me around, pointed me
towards the stage and shoved me out there with such force that
I stumbled onstage giving the Nazi salute (the raised right hand
was actually there to break my fall).

Hen's book exudes, with charm and whimsy, a sort of pratfall
attitude to life, something she has slightly in common with me
– that's why we were such fun together and why she was such a
great tour manager for me Oh, it was *hysterical*. As in the case
of the infamous pork-chop incident. Where was that?
Somewhere in Ireland. Sligo, perhaps. I was a bit out of control
and having Hen as my minder wasn't all that helpful in
keeping the lid on things, so I was quite wild and unpredictable
and high and drunk much of the time on that tour. I was
drunk when I came on stage and someone in the audience
threw a pork chop at me. I ducked and it hit my guitar player
Joe Maverty right in the head! As you know, I *have* behaved
awfully badly in my day. No one would argue with that, I think
– least of all me. But I haven't done that sort of thing for a *long*
time!

And after that tour we needed to relax, didn't we? I spent a
wonderful time with her in Jamaica for six months. We stayed
at the Runaway Bay Hotel – it should've been called the Runaway
Bill Hotel, actually – having the greatest, wildest time together.
Henrietta was drinking zombies made with four different types
of rum, all 170 proof. It's a wonder she didn't just evaporate!
But she was made of very stern stuff indeed. I was drinking
vodka and grapefruit juice like there was no tomorrow – and as

far as we were concerned, there wasn't. Hen was shagging the band leader, we were hanging out with flamboyant gay blacks who the hotel for some reason didn't care for. We weren't doing anything *that* dreadful, but I'm sure we were so not the kind of clients they were trying to cultivate. We were there for a month and then we had to leave. Asked to leave, pushed out the door, essentially. They got fed up with us and wouldn't have us any longer, so we went to Sally and Perry Henzell's.

Poor Chris Blackwell had to go and pay the bill, which was vast and huge. They piled it on. Chris was furious about having to pay this monstrous bill, at the same time adoring Hen and me. That kind of conflict is always fun, don't you think? I hung my head and beat my breast in shame, but fucking hell I had a good time. And, in fact, *I* ended up paying for it all out of my royalties, but at the time I believed Chris was nobly picking up the tab out of love and respect for two great broads.

Brilliant, funny Hen; foul-mouthed, amoral, a thief, a violent drunkard and a drug addict, but she was witty, wonderfully warm and lovable, and she had a good heart. A lot of times when I was really in deep shit, like when I was in New York on heroin hanging around Frin's house, really in a bad way, Hen would come over and look after me. She was incredibly kind-hearted and she loved me, I don't know why. She'd do very simple things that would reduce me to tears, like making me scrambled eggs on toast with a bit of parsley on the side.

Hen was one of the freest people I've ever known. A lot of people talk the high loon talk on the King's Road or on

Glastonbury Tor, but very few people could *embody* it – the moment, the time, the let's-drop-everything-and-do-thisness of Henrietta. She was the greatest company and just about the funniest person I've ever met. She could go off on the nature of the tomato, its colour, roundness, history, symbolism. How it was 'just perfection, and, would you believe it? Comes with seeds so when you're done with it you can just plant them and grow twenty more.' A tomato could in her prolix rap turn into a metaphor for the meaning of life.

'Erratic, neurotic, demanding, devious, and fickle,' she wrote of herself in her autobiography. Typical of Hen to omit *entirely* all her noble attributes: caring, clever, loyal, loving, witty, enthusiastic to a fault. As filled as her life was with famous, notorious, brilliant people, almost as much space in her memoir is devoted to dogs, from brindled lurchers to German shepherds to greyhounds and mutts.

I did see her towards the end and I could see she was very, very ill, and I'm sure she knew it. That's why all her friends got together at that point, really, and more or less *forced* her to write her memoir, because her life was so riveting, the two dykes and Simla and all that. My favourite line in *Henrietta* is when she calls Marina Guinness 'Desmond's darling daughter'. I can just see her, sitting there, pondering that line, you know, because it's really a double-edged sword.

Hen had lovely dogs. There were some lovely little dachshunds, but they were very nervy and a bit damaged – rather like their mistress. Dogs definitely do pick up their owners' traits and some people even start looking like their animals. I don't know if Hen looked like a dachshund exactly, but inside there must have been something. My mother's dog, who outlived her a little while, died of the same thing she did – it had a bad heart. So if I have a dog, heaven help it!

Hen's memoirs ramble on a bit – which is perfectly appropriate, perfectly Henrietta. Part of it is just very bread-and-butter descriptions of things and people, then suddenly there's all these mad scenes. The cat burglar business, looking for the Holy Grail, the amphetamine psychosis story – that's *so* funny!

Hen was very, very loved. She was fun to be with, but did have a very grumpy side to her which manifested itself quite startlingly in a character she called Scotch Jimmy. Scotch Jimmy was a demon that appeared when she got really drunk and nasty. I never saw Scotch Jimmy myself – he only began to appear near the very end, in the last two years.

Hen came to Christmas dinner one year and was really highly rated by François, because he'd brought some pâté de foie gras from the Dordogne that his mother had made herself and Hen was the only person there who understood what it was, because, despite her knock-about life, she was very sophisticated, she knew about all that sort of thing. She had learned a lot from Francis Bacon. Francis knew his food, I can tell you. I got to know him well when I was living on my wall. Nobody knew where I was, really, except for Francis, who came across me one day and said: 'You look like you need a meal!' And took me to Wheelers and I had a lovely time and then we started to talk a little bit.

You can't imagine how much Henrietta taught me! About *Les Enfants du Paradis* – French movies, avant-garde theatre, art – things that changed my world, *rocked* my world. To be so close to somebody like that was inspiring.

I was able to help her out a bit in her last phase. I bought Henrietta a set of teeth. She'd started drinking again and somehow she had some kind of fall or someone punched her and she had her teeth knocked out and nobody was prepared to do anything about it. Henrietta, as you can see on the cover of her book, had been a really great beauty, and a face without your front teeth – it's just all caved in – and so I bought her some teeth and sent her to a good dentist and, hopefully, she got the teeth I wanted her to get, but I don't think she did. I think she got cheap teeth and then spent the rest of the money on booze. At the end she had serious cirrhosis.

In the last year of Henrietta's life the artist Maggi Hambling looked after her and the two of them collaborated on a series of Expressionist portraits. 'However arthritic or, on occasion, hung over,' Hambling wrote in *Maggi and Henrietta*, 'she gallantly climbed onto the table to pose: raw, intense, vulnerable and commanding. I became her subject rather than she mine. Her inspiration for me was a powerful mixture of attack, encouragement and wit.' And in an act that Hen would have considered the greatest act of friendship, Maggi took care of her beloved dog after she died.

Towards the end of her life Hen had taken to gardening with the same zeal with which she had embraced methedrine, cat burglary and all her other mad-cap adventures. I have to end with her description of the garden she created, which is so lyrical and personal it's as if the flowers in her hands came to life – which is just what they did:

> The garden progressed much in the way that I had planned. Snowdrops gave way to daffodils and then primroses, violets, tulips, wallflowers, and by summer everything was in full bloom. The 'Gloire de Dijon' opened up into great globules of pale pinkish yellow touched with gold at the centre. The 'Albertine' and the 'Mermaid' twined lovingly into the trellis of the pergola and a large, double-flowered white clematis and a honeysuckle climbed up alongside them. Lupins, foxgloves and hollyhocks nodded imperially at each other, and yellow Welsh poppies and celestially blue Himalayan poppies provided pools of colour. There were also groups of white marguerites and several bush roses bought on the spur of the moment at Covent Garden. Along the edge of the curved bed, set in among the old brick edging, yellow and purple violas jostled each other, while in the Versailles pots on the pergola steps clumps of 'Bowles' Black' violets looked mysteriously back at me, nestling down among the roots of the roses.

I adored her.

donatella versace

I never got to know Gianni Versace but some years ago I happened to be in New York and there was a huge exhibition of Versace designs at the Metropolitan Museum, with a big dinner and gala after the show. I went with Kate Moss, who was wearing a beautiful old Versace number that she owned, and I was dressed by the House in one of their new creations. It was the most amazing, glittering night out; it was that kind of do. But the real fun began afterwards, when a few of us went back to the Versace house with Donatella, whom I had never met before. There was me and Kate, and Rupert Everett and Cher, and a guy called Antonio who I think was one of Donatella's cutters, plus a handful of people I didn't know. The Versace house in New York was exactly what I had imagined: Nero's Palace, impossibly grand and Romanesque. We were all there in evening dress in the middle of this hard New York winter, and yet in the house we could wander about barefoot, what with the central heating under the mosaic floor tiles. We ended up having a sort of wake for Gianni. After everybody left, me, Kate, Donatella, Antonio and Cher sat around talking about death and drinking champagne.

Kate decided that this should be a real wake and that we all had to sing. I sang an old Irish folk song and Donatella cried. And then Kate turned to Cher and said it was her turn to sing. I've known Cher for many years; I first met her when we appeared on the TV rock show *Shindig* together back in the sixties. She's a wonderful and genuine person, but not exactly spontaneous. So here we were in Nero's Palace, draped over these Romanesque couches all covered with Gianni's leopardskin fabrics, in a vast marble hall with high fluted columns, fountains and fresco'd ceilings. And Cher stood up in all her glory, and my God she was amazing, plastic surgery or not, dressed in this astounding figure-hugging green Versace. She looked like a supernatural being, unearthly and breathtaking. With her hair down to her waist, a siren from Greek mythology standing before us in this fabulous temple. She stood there and sang 'Danny Boy'; her voice, echoing through the colonnades and resonating somewhere high above us on the gilded ceiling, was spine-tingling. Of course by the time she finished we were all sobbing, even Antonio the cutter. We couldn't take our eyes off her.

sixties legend in death plunge

My frock mania may or may not be a curable virus, but little did I think that my fashion fetish might actually be *fatal*. Read on . . .

A beautiful Irish spring day in 2000, with François and I finalising arrangements for our holiday in Jamaica. Dan and Rebecca Day Lewis were coming to dinner, so we were excited about that too. François was cooking, and I had gone out and bought some really lovely wine at Oddbins up the road. Daniel doesn't drink, but Rebecca likes a glass of wine, as does François and, of course, yours truly.

As evening approached I got dressed, putting on my green dress and black body stocking, red fishnet tights, and red Christian Louboutin shoes. These particular red shoes were given to me when I did a photo shoot; Christian makes the shoes that I'm always going on about, you know, the ones where even the soles are red (albeit not for very long).

I had a few odds and ends that I wanted to wash before the trip, so I traipsed upstairs to the washing machine room in my high heels and loaded the thing. I was wrapped up in one of my usual daydreams. I usually limit myself to forgetting to put in the soap or putting it in twice, but what with the big trip ahead, I was bound to do something really spectacular. As I came down the stairs, the little rubber thing on the end of the heel somehow caught on the carpet and over I went, sailing through the air down the stairs. It was surreal, with everything switching into the slow motion one always hears about, except this motion was *really* slow. I mean, when people say your life flashes before your eyes, I didn't realise they meant that the movie takes an hour. I've since talked about this to Tarka Cordell and he said the very same thing happened to him when he came off a motorbike. I could see myself slowly falling down the stairs, and as I fell I could see that I was going to break my neck and die. The surprising thing was that I seemed to have a lot of time to think about this, weighing the pros and cons, and deciding that, no, I didn't want to break my neck because I was really quite happy with my lot in life. So at fifty I made a conscious decision to turn my body in mid air and put my shoulder forward to take the fall, thus saving my neck. I was only able to be so agile because it happened so very slowly.

Well, I've never had such a pain in my entire life, a white searing pain, after which I literally saw stars. There I was, back in my body, crumpled up at the bottom of the stairs. I started to yell. It was all so peculiar; I'd fallen on to my shoulder so all I could do was to roll on to my back, which I don't even remember doing. I just remember coming round a bit and desperately squawking out for help. François was there and he couldn't believe it. I can still see his face looking down at me, white as a sheet. And I can remember seeing my skirt, all green with red fishnets coming out of it. It was a strange detachment, me looking at this frozen image of myself at the bottom of the stairs with my legs pointing upwards. God, it was so awful, and of course François was freaking. But thank God he was there, because I couldn't move at all; there is absolutely no way that I could have crawled out of the stairwell and opened the door to reach the phone. If François had been away, I guess I could have died right there. What an embarrassing way to go! Not the death any of us picture for ourselves. Drug overdose: classic tacky. Ham sandwich: hard to live down. Drowning: suspicious. But falling down the stairs because your heels are too high? The vanity! The klutziness! Perhaps the shame is actually what saved me.

Anyway François called the ambulance and it arrived within five minutes. Oh, Jesus! Cute young ambulance guys! I'm not ready for this. Again I got the feeling of how weird I looked, all crumpled up in these smart clothes and red stockings, the shoes left tragically on the stairs rather like the pair in the window in Michael Powell's film *The Red Shoes*. I knew that I had broken my shoulder, but obviously the cute ambulance men didn't know, and so they took no chances, strapping me on to a stretcher, and putting a collar on me even though I told them I didn't need it (it didn't go with my outfit). They were brilliant and so nice, and fussing about over me terribly. God knows how they got me down the stairs; I tried to think about something else: reciting *The Rime of the Ancient Mariner* in my mind, and oddly trying to figure out whether Excalibur was the sword in the stone or the one the Lady in the Lake held up.

At St Vincent's Hospital I had to wait two hours on the stretcher, which was placed on a trolley, and all this without painkillers. Eventually I was given some pethidine, and then X-rays were taken. The break was serious but clean. And then they just put me in a sling and sent me home. There was talk about perhaps putting pins into my arm, but having seen what they did to Penny Guinness when she broke her hip, there was no way I was going to let them do that. I knew then that I was lucky with such a clean break, and I felt strangely exhilarated. Now it was just a case of staying in bed for a couple of weeks. And, of course, no Jamaica.

I slept an awful lot, and went into shock. John and Sarah Hurt came round and did some shopping for us. Sleep was just about all I could manage; I couldn't even think, let alone read. I just dozed and watched stupid things on day-time television; I'd be vaguely aware of *The Love Boat* or *Falcon Crest* or some such programme. But in the evenings I'd feel much better; I'd up the ante to *Friends* and *ER*, and I really got into *Sabrina the Teenage Witch*, which I now love. Having always been a fan of *Bewitched* way back when, it was a true delight to discover *Sabrina* and her two sexy aunts, not to mention the talking cat. And may I add that it's a much better show than *Buffy the Vampire Slayer,* in case the reader is interested in such telly arcana.

During this period, I was not the best patient in the world. Or rather, I was good at being a patient. François's birthday came and went and I managed to do nothing about it at all. I just lay there thinking what a complete bummer it was: me in bed with a broken shoulder and we're meant to be in Jamaica. Boo-hoo. A very blue day indeed. We cheered ourselves up watching Woody Allen's *Sweet and Lowdown*. It hurt me to laugh, but I just had to. Sean Penn's performance! And the young English actress who plays the mute girl! Quite astonishing. The way the Penn character gets his kicks from shooting the rats in the rubbish tips just broke me up. The movie is a small masterpiece . . . a real gem.

My first day out it took me nearly three hours to get dressed. It was a lunch at John Boorman's house in Anamoe. Dear Isabella threw a belated gathering for François's birthday, the lunch was delicious, and John got out some of his finest wine, followed by a very good vintage port. Geoffrey Rush, Gareth Brown and Jamie Lee Curtis were amongst the guests and I hoped we were making it up to François. Geoffrey took me for a little walk to John's Japanese garden. John had just finished shooting *The Tailor of Panama*, and everyone was very excited; Jamie and Geoffrey bubbling over, John always calm, but they all had a feeling that the movie was going to be really good, which it turned out to be.

At lunch, I found out that on the Sunday after my accident all the papers had been running with headlines like '60s LEGEND IN DEATH PLUNGE'. Apparently it was wild because you couldn't tell from the headline that I *wasn't* dead. I guess the papers got hold of the story from the hospital. Isabella told me that they had made a shrine for me in their house using pictures from the newspapers as well as other pictures that they had around.

After lunch, I got to see the shrine that they had made for my 'death'. It was built in the conservatory with pictures from the tabloids, all centred on the screaming '60s LEGEND IN DEATH PLUNGE!' caption. It was all pinned up on canvas with flowers all around and acupuncture pins nailed to my shoulder in the photos. Some lovely psychic healing in a sort of Mexican shrine, that mad South American mixture of Catholicism and paganism. As I had seen hardly any of the newspaper stories about my fall, I found it all quite amazing. Mad; they had really gone to town on it. I felt like Tom Sawyer at his own funeral.

decadence as a fine art

My new theory about decadence and all that stuff – is that it's an *idea*. You don't have to act it out, you can just fantasise.

I actually do have a strong decadent streak. It's genetic, from my great uncle Leopold Sacher-Masoch. But I don't actually have to *do* anything to emanate that feeling. I don't have to take drugs, I don't have to drink, I don't have to be promiscuous. I certainly don't have to dress up in whips and chains and get thrashed like my poor uncle Leopold. Masochism is a very sad perversion as far as sexual deviance goes – to only be able to have an orgasm when somebody's beating the shit out of you.

What I've come up with is that decadence is mostly a concept and it can be in you and part of you without involving all the usual culprits: sex and drugs and alcohol. If you read that classic text of decadence, Huysmans' *À Rebours (Against Nature)*, you'll notice it's not about any of that. Its protagonist, Des Esseintes, is an eccentric, reclusive aesthete who sets gemstones in the shell of his turtle, decorates his house with medieval thumbscrews and garrottes instead of pictures. But it's all in his mind. He

doesn't *use* them, he just looks at them. The decadence comes
from the extreme (and provocatively perverse) point of view
that the artificial is far more appealing than the organic.
'Artifice, besides, seemed to Des Esseintes the final distinctive
mark of man's genius,' Huysmans writes.

> Nature had had her day, as he put it. By the disgusting
> sameness of her landscapes and skies, she had once and for
> all wearied the considerate patience of aesthetes. Is there a
> woman, whose form is more dazzling, more splendid than
> the two locomotives that pass over the Northern Railroad
> lines? One, the Crampton, is an adorable, shrill-voiced
> blonde . . . The other, the Engerth, is a nobly proportioned
> dusky brunette emitting raucous, muffled cries.

There's nothing destructive or sinister about this form of
decadence. On the contrary, it's a creative way of seeing things
that playfully inverts the platitudes that numb the brain and lets
us look at the world anew.

a giant musical mouse

In 2000 I had a great time recording 'Love Got Lost' on Joe Jackson's *Night and Day II* album. At first he was jet-lagged and seemed quite shy. With his pale skin, white eyebrows and eyelashes, he resembled a giant musical mouse. It took me right back to my childhood when I used to keep pet mice. I especially remember two called Daphne and Chloë – I always gave my mice Greek names, and would bring them to school. So, being well up on the mouse vibe very much endeared Joe to me. He's a charming man, very much a pro musician, and I made him laugh a lot telling him stories about Van the Man Morrison, and thumbnail sketches of mad musical life in Dublin.

Joe particularly loved the stories of Van going into those little houses in the back streets of King's Cross with the writer Mick Brown looking for swamis and gurus and whatnot. Brown's wonderful book *The Spiritual Tourist* begins: 'I suppose it was in the autumn of 1984 when I got a call from Van asking whether I wanted to meet a man who claimed to know the whereabouts of Christ.' And on they go in search of Christ the Redeemer in the East End, now having morphed into a Hindu entity called

Maitreya who allegedly ministers to mini-cab drivers and sweatshop workers. They also visit swamis in bed-sits who magically out of thin air sprinkle their palms with *vibhuti* (ashes from burnt cow dung).

gregory corso

Christmas. Ireland. 2000. The phone rings. It's Gregory, my old dear friend, Gregory Corso, last of the great Beat poets. 'Darling,' the familiar croaky voice with a ripe New York accent says, 'I think I'm fading. I think I'm gonna go soon. You'd better get here!'

'God, Gregory, I can't get there till January,' I say.

'Babe, I don't think I'm going to be able to make it to January.'

'Gregory, I can't, I just can't. You have to not croak until I get there. Do not croak until January the second!'

'Okay, it might be difficult,' he says with stoic resignation. 'But I'll try.'

And, bugger me, he waited, and croaked a month later! Gregory lived just long enough! Wasn't that noble? The nobility of soul there! Good God, what a pro.

In January 2001 I went with my old friend Hal Willner –
curator of souls, hipster, producer of miraculous albums – to
Gregory's daughter's house in Minnesota to make an album of
Gregory's work. *Die On Me* it's called. Every day we'd go over
to work with Gregory. He was very ill. It was very sad, because
he'd always been so full of life.

It wasn't all that comfortable for us being there. We were part
of his spiritual family but we weren't relatives and we were
putting Gregory – who was clearly about to die any day –
under a lot of stress. Nevertheless Gregory wanted us there
more than anything.

I still feel his spirit was so formed by his prison and
reformatory experiences, where he always had a cramped
little area wherever he lived, shut off from everything,
very small, where he wrote, and that's why he needed to be
alone so much. He wasn't a group guy at all. Unlike Allen, for
example.

When I think of Gregory sitting alone in his room writing,
I always think of Hamlet's line: 'I could be bounded in a
nutshell, and count myself a king of infinite space, were it
not that I have bad dreams.' Those monk-like spaces in
prison and reform school made him a poet in some way
because they made him happy to be in a room on his own and
not see anybody and read and write and I guess get high.
'Sometimes hell is a good place,' he wrote, 'if it proves to one
that because it exists, so must its opposite, heaven, exist. And
what is heaven? Poetry.' Ordinarily he couldn't do social

situations all that well. But this time, those four days that Hal and I spent with him, he was in great form and in complete control of the session.

I just want to go back a bit to where all this started. After Hal did Allen Ginsberg's record, *Holy Soul Jelly Roll*, Allen said to him, 'Why don't you do Gregory?' Allen was always bringing his friends in, the way he did his whole life. I knew Gregory from for ever, but Hal wasn't that familiar with his work. When he was researching Allen's *Holy Soul Jelly Roll* boxed set, Hal came across a bunch of tapes of Gregory from the late fifties and early sixties when he did most of his classic readings. He became a brilliant reader of his own work, a put-on artist, mumbling random surrealisms into the microphone ('all life is a rotary club', 'I found God a gigantic fly paper', 'fish is animalised water'), a shock-troop poet in an increasingly shockproof avant-garde.

> *It's all abnormal!*
> *The virgin is sick!*
> *The whore is sick!*
> *The Cocksucker the cuntlapper, sick!*
> *The sodomist the normalist, sick!*
> *The celibate the cocksman, sick!*
> *Yes! Every man & woman who ever fucked, sick!*
> *The fucked and the fuckers*
> *The unfucked and the non-fuckers, SICK!*
> *To the gas-chamber with all of them!*
>
> from 'On Chessman's Crime'

Allen always said that Gregory was the best one, the best performer of that whole era. He was unbelievable to listen to when he was reading 'Marriage' and 'Bomb!' and those early poems. 'Bomb!' is one of the most amazing poems from the entire Beat canon, a mano-a-mano bar brawl with the atomic bomb:

> *Budger of history Brake of time You Bomb*
> *Toy of universe Grandest of all snatched-sky I cannot hate you*
> *Do I hate the mischievous thunderbolt the jawbone of an ass*
> *The bumpy club of One Million B.C. the mace the flail the axe*
> *Catapult Da Vinci tomahawk Cochise flintlock Kidd dagger*
> *Rathbone*
> *Ah and the sad desperate gun of Verlaine Pushkin Dillinger*
> *Bogart*
> *And hath not St Michael a burning sword St George a lance*
> *David a sling*
> *Bomb you are as cruel as man makes you and you're no crueller*
> *than cancer . . .*

Later on, Gregory didn't have Allen's organisational skill – Allen was always categorising, filing, cataloguing – and he didn't, like Burroughs, have a James Grauerholz, a disciple to keep him together. After Hal first approached him about doing his album, Gregory spent three years avoiding doing the record. Then he got prostate cancer, and Hal and I thought we'd better go over and see Gregory. This was when he was still living over on Horatio Street in New York. It was terrible, he couldn't talk, his eyes were black. It looked like the end, and we thought, 'Oh shit, we're too late.'

But then he had a remission – that's when he called me, and I think what partly got this thing going again was our unconsummated forty-year romance. Suddenly Gregory started saying, 'When are we going to do my record?' Shortly after that he went to live with his daughter in Minnesota. It was very difficult because by the time we arrived he'd become ill again.

There was Gregory in hospital clothes sitting in a chaise. He was so lucky, in many ways, because his daughter, Sheri Langerman, whom he hardly knew, whom he'd almost forgotten, reappeared in his life out of the blue when he got cancer. She was a nurse, no less, and took care of him at home until his death. He was in a bed on a morphine pump – there are a lot of morphine pumps in my world – but it wasn't working very well. What I found out about this shocked me. If you shoot smack all your life, when you are really ill, the receptor cells that the drug hangs on to don't respond, so you don't get that rush of dopamine; it doesn't quell the pain. It was terrible to see somebody I loved being so ill. Apart from my parents going through their illnesses, it was the most intense pain I've ever had to witness.

We were taping works of his from when he was young, so it was very emotional. It was heavy. Gregory and I would talk about mythology and Keats and Shelley and Milton, Gilgamesh and Dionysus. It was charming and touching, and Hal was recording it all. If he turned the tape recorder off, Gregory would sit up and say, 'Turn it on; I want to read. Turn it on; I want to talk.'

Gregory's searchlight was very narrow. It wasn't like Allen's world poetry anthology, it didn't cover from everything to everything, from Walt Whitman to haiku. You didn't get those kinds of books in prison. Very simple: Byron, Keats, Shelley, finis. Until he met the boys, that was it. An incredible kind of training, isn't it? Straight out of the 1820s into 1950s America.

Gregory was very ruthless in that last week. Ruthless about his work, what pieces he wanted to read and what he wanted me to read and how he wanted it done and very conscious of himself as a great poet. It was hard work. I was so fond of him – not everybody was. Gregory wasn't to everybody's taste. He was very difficult and, when he got drunk, he could be a terror (although he was always very sweet with me). We had this strange romance, me and Gregory. A strange intellectual romance, although Gregory never let a minute pass, even when he was on his deathbed, where he wasn't trying to make a pass.

Hal had done a record with William Burroughs, *Dead City Radio,* on which he'd got Bill to read things other than his own work. He got Bill to do the Lord's Prayer and all sorts of strange things. Just weird stuff. That's how Hal is. But Gregory didn't want that at all. It was his poetry and he wanted to have his poetry sound good. He wanted only the Corso opus. I think he was absolutely right.

It was incredibly sweet of Gregory to let me be involved in his last spoken testament. He let me read his poem on Brigitte Bardot. Allen wouldn't have let me do that, nor would

Burroughs. But Gregory was looser, more democratic – and idiosyncratic. Considering he was a week away from dying, it was pretty impressive that he had the strength to do the record at all. He'd obviously been thinking about it for a long time.

Hal was a bit afraid of Gregory – in the way that one who didn't know him too well would be – because Gregory was so smart. He was self-educated and phenomenally literate. He'd quote something from Shelley and if you didn't recognise it he dismissed you.

Gregory had a very impish sense of humour – he drove poor Allen barking mad. Well, you can imagine how cross Allen would get with Gregory's wild antics! Gregory was such fun and, bad though he was, he wasn't *that* bad – and even when he was, he was worth it. Outrageous beyond belief what he does to this kid in *When I Was Cool*. It's just, like, psychic rape or something! He could be very difficult. He was like some doped-up thug, but in a sweet way, and he did have that side to him. He wasn't in jail for nothing. Gregory could be absolutely appalling, no question about that. He just surpassed himself on the level of bad behaviour, even by his own standards!

But then again, Gregory was so lovable! And such a hustler! But I am glad I didn't, despite his insistence, give in to his wheedling and bring any coke down for him as he asked me to do. It really wouldn't have been good form. But I know how tempting that can be. When he was stronger, I could have just said: 'Oh, fuck off, Gregory! Please! Give me a break!' And he would have stopped, but he was so sick and so desperate. That last week was so hard and one of the hardest things was when he said to me: 'Did you bring me any coke?' and I hadn't.

'Oh, Marianne, *why* didn't you? *Why*, babe? You *know* how *bad* I need it.' That voice! I can't do the New York accent, but all this was said in that moany, rusty voice. Whine, whine, whine. But it would not have been a nice thing to do to his daughter. Of course, there was a little part of me that thought, 'Oh, I should have done!' Because he wanted it so badly.

I first met Gregory with Allen Ginsberg in Paris in the sixties. I went to see him with my husband John Dunbar circa 1964. He was a grand old man of the Beat Generation by then, though all of thirty-three, I should think. He was living in his garret-like room, very *la vie bohème*. He did a good Stanley Kowalski. When he was young it was white T-shirts and jeans, obviously, and he looked fantastic. He'd mutter inscrutable asides, the way he did at his readings: 'Holy communion or basketball?' 'Chameleons eat light and air' – that sort of thing. I was absolutely terrified. We'd not been there five minutes when he promptly drank a whole bottle of the Brompton Mixture and passed out. It's a concoction of heroin and cocaine that they used to prescribe for cancer patients in England. Outrageous! But one expected no less of a genius poet. I was terribly impressed.

I remember thinking that Gregory was mad and scary, quite unlike Allen. Allen was the approachable, cuddly and loving face of the Beat Generation. But Gregory and Burroughs I found absolutely terrifying. Much later, when I got to know them, I discovered that they were not at all what I thought.

Burroughs was odd, of course, and at that time he would have had no interest at all in pretty little girls like me; there was nothing about me that Burroughs would have been even *remotely* interested in; he wouldn't have been aware of me even if I'd been in the same room as him. But unlike Allen and Bill, Gregory wasn't gay.

Gregory was the youngest of the Beat poets, discovered by Ginsberg, who got him published. Ginsberg had anointed him, calling him 'a great word-swinger, first naked sign of a poet, a scientific master of mad mouthfuls of language'. Gregory had a life-long smack habit, which affected his ability to work. I take out his book and read his poems every now and again, and he's still amazing – the dark horse of the Beats; the one about whom little is known.

At that time in the sixties when I first met the alpha Beats, Burroughs was the outstanding one among them, and the one whose work I liked the most. Later I went to many readings of Allen's work, and I realised what a great poet he was; but secretly tucked away in Horatio Street, Gregory Corso was beavering away, producing this wonderful canon of work that is arguably, in retrospect, as good as any the Beats produced.

I knew Gregory over a very long period of time and each time I saw him he was different, which I always found surprising. At the same time, I was rather pleased, because one of the most boring things about people, one of the saddest things about human beings in general, is that once you get a picture of them in your mind's eye, however awful or however wonderful it is, as life goes on, you can't seem to change that picture – and neither can they. They're incapable of seeing that this version of themselves doesn't work any more (rarely do they update it). But Gregory wasn't like that at all.

I'm hanging on by the skin of my teeth, but I do believe that sometimes people can evolve – and that was Gregory. Gregory evolved, Gregory multiplied into many different Gregories. You're very lucky if you can evolve, because there are people walking around who aren't even human, maybe, they're still dogs, and not nice ones.

Gregory's drug habits were his personal demon; he didn't feel it was his mission to turn the world on to heroin. I don't know how he felt about his habit, but I doubt he felt that great about it.

I saw him again at a poetry meeting in Westminster Abbey and he was a different man altogether. I was one of the few people he knew there that day. He was dressed in a suit and looked very elegant. I could see he was nervous, which told me he wasn't high or drunk. He was clean. He'd decided to try and get through it without being high. That was a long, long time ago.

He'd always been a flash dresser, even in his Stanley Kowalski mode, but later on I was surprised to find him decked out in designer clothes. He greeted François and me dressed in this gorgeous Agnès B. Homme suit. Very smart, the whole suit was a dark mushroom velvet. He'd been flirting with me for thirty years and always held out the promise of writing me a poem. I guess the time had come, because there it was, very beautiful and clearly something he'd worked on and crafted, called 'Sing a Sad Song'. There's a bit that goes: 'Soon the shadows of sleep will be bereft of music's marrow/And clanking skeletons shall jounce their wend/toward the bassoon men.' I'm sure that's him, that bit.

Hal compares Gregory to a cross between Stan Laurel and W. C. Fields with a touch of Lon Chaney. 'I myself am my own happy fool,' he wrote of himself in 'Clown'; an image Kerouac, in his conclusion to *The Subterraneans*, would agree with: '. . . but I continue the daydream and I look in his eyes and I suddenly see the glare of a jester angel who made his presence on earth all a joke . . . and I think "Funny Angel, elevated amongst the subterraneans."'

It was a very difficult time. We were in a house of death, but when I hear Gregory laughing while I'm reading his poetry on the album – which you *must* get! – I see Gregory rise up with his wicked puckish grin, a wild jail kid, but so sweet.

Out of everybody's hearing I whispered to him, 'Now, Gregory, when you get there, let me know something.' Terrible of me! He looked at me and said, 'Darling, I won't be able to do that. But if I can, I will.'

After four days of Gregory reading, soliloquising, quoting the immortals, and gossiping, we left. A week after we'd finished making the album, Gregory died, on 19th January 2001. He was seventy years old. He wanted his ashes to be sprinkled in the same place where Shelley drowned in the Gulf of Spezia because he loved Shelley so much.

Nobody listened to the tapes until a year later. Michael Minzer, who financed the album, started listening to the tapes and editing them and there was great stuff on them. The record made itself. Hal cut between takes of Gregory when he was younger, where he's singing and telling his stories and talking, and Gregory when we recorded him in Minnesota. He added some strings, Laurie Anderson did some overdub, and there you have it: this wonderful visit with Gregory.

sex with strangers and other guilty pleasures

Kissin' Time is much lighter, much more Pop than anything I've done since the sixties, and, in a very deliberate way, it's sixties retro.

I dreamt up the project on New Year's Eve 2000, at Dan Macmillan's flat looking at that amazing fireworks display over the Thames. I suddenly felt inspired. 'Marianne, it's high time you did something new,' a little voice was saying to me. 'Stop writing songs about the past! Change everything!' Probably the magic mushrooms talking, but that's what they're there for, isn't it?

I also realised then that I would need real help to do this, so I made a little list in my head. Instead of my going to those old war-horses like Keith Richards, which is what I've always done before, I decided instead to work with much younger people.

With *Kissin' Time*, I said to François, 'I want to do something completely different. I want to make a happy record, celebrating love and life.' François looked at me like I'd lost my mind, but he just said, 'Make a wish list of who you'd like to work with. We'll ring them up and see.' Well, we did, and they all said yes. First up was Damon Albarn of Blur whom I knew a bit. And Alex James, Blur's bass player, who's a good mate of mine, too. I know their music and it was exactly the kind of thing I wanted to have on my record. And then Pulp popped into my head. I really like Jarvis Cocker, great, witty, quirky kitchen-sink lyrics.

I made *Kissin' Time* with Damon Albarn, Billy Corgan, Jarvis Cocker and Beck. It came out of mutual love of each other's music. It would never have happened without it. There's a form of intense fandom that radiates throughout the record. Writing with other people doesn't, of course, always turn out as blissfully as you'd like; people often aren't who you thought they were. So you're amazed in another way entirely – the *wrong* way. I worked with someone like that and we did actually make a good song, but he was ghastly. A complete monomaniac.

But, I mean, everybody is a bit of an egomaniac in this biz, aren't they? I take that as par for the course in any creative writing situation. Well, you're bound to be a bit. Otherwise you wouldn't be doing this insane stuff in front of thousands of people.

Of course, if you hate the music they come up with, you tend to not say anything. In case you're wondering what to do when that happens, you just say, 'Thank you. We'll be in touch.'

Anyway, the *fun* we had working together reminded me a lot of the way Mick and Keith worked. Keith is very evolved in that way; he can put his ego to one side. But in the sixties, most people couldn't do that, really. Now we're able to leave some of our ego at the door and do the work. Maybe it's old age!

One evening I got a surprise phone call from Billy Corgan of the Smashing Pumpkins saying that his band were playing in the Olympia Theatre at 8 p.m. and wondering if I would like to come. For once in my life I answered Yes! without hesitating. And let me get this on the record: the gig was absolutely fucking wonderful. Billy, whom I'd never seen or met before, was wearing a dress and Doc Martens, and with his baldy head he was the most *extraordinary* sight. He also sings and plays guitar like you wouldn't believe. Just brilliant. It takes a special kind of freak to do what Billy does. Any old guitar wally can put on tight jeans and a leather jacket, but Billy Corgan is something else altogether. So afterwards I went backstage to pay my respects, and I found myself saying, 'Would it be possible for us to get together and do something?' I knew that I was heading to LA soon and he immediately said, 'Yes!' and then looked François straight in the eye and said, 'I'm not the kind of person who says something and doesn't mean it.'

Broken English was very electronic – we were just twenty-two years ahead of the equipment. So one of the reasons I wanted to make *Kissin' Time* was because I realised that there were all these new instruments and technologies I didn't know about – and I like to be in on the beginning of things.

'Wherever I Go', which precedes 'Song for Nico' (me and Dave Stewart), is almost a mock mid-sixties pop song, like you might hear on a soundtrack to an Audrey Hepburn movie. It came about when Billy Corgan decided what I needed was a proper album-oriented rock hit, so we wrote a love song.

They all knew my early work, and, apart from 'Nobody's Fault', all the songs relate to that period of my life. What all these guys who worked with me on the album did was to pretend that after 1966 I disappeared completely. Never ran away with Mick Jagger; never became a junkie; never did any of that; never wrote 'Sister Morphine'; never made *Broken English*; never did anything after 'As Tears Go By'. And then, like Sleeping Beauty, I suddenly reappeared with *Kissin' Time*, as if nothing happened. They just wiped out the whole middle-eight of my life. Not to deny it because, of course, it *did* happen, but what I'm trying to say is that they are just sort of as-if stories. What we did is impossible, of course. If I hadn't run off with Mick, not written 'Sister Morphine', not this, not that – all those nots – I could not have made this record. They are all connected. But still, that is the illusion, and it is a beautiful one. The lovely little folky Beck song 'Like Being Born' is the same sort of thing really.

'Like Being Born' isn't exactly about my family. Only the first verse is about my parents. 'My father promised me roses, my mother promised me thorns, like being born.' The second half is about my lover. 'He touches me lightly with his hand – it feels like being born.' That is not my father, obviously. On this track I was trying to use my voice as if it were an interior historian chronicling the seismic shifts in my life. That was the idea, anyway, but I never discussed that with anyone. And, to tell you the truth, I didn't quite know what it was about myself! I don't always know what songs are about when I write them. And sometimes they don't just come, sometimes I have to really *slog*.

On 'I'm on Fire' I give the word 'happiness' a kind of gothic patina, because it's a word so overused you need to put a bit of a spin on it. It's a word I've never said in a song before. I don't know where it came from. It was just a moment; that's all a song is – a flash. It's not the facts, the truth, for ever. I didn't know what was coming. If you'd said the word happiness to me three weeks earlier, I would've thrown up! Happiness and no more pain, hah! I'm much better now, thank you. I'm fine.

'Sliding Through Life on Charm' I did with Pulp, whose records I really like. So cute, Pulp playing to all the British trees. When they said they were going to do a tour for all the ancient forests of Britain and Brittany and Ireland, I actually imagined they were going to play *just* to the trees. They brought me back to earth, saying, 'Well, Marianne, there *will* actually be *people* there, too.' What an idea! There are some of us left.

Trees and music are an ancient pair. There used to be the Tree of Hope at the Apollo Theater in Harlem. It was the trunk of the tree that actors in the old days would stand under when they were looking for parts. In the thirties it got cut down, and they took the trunk of this tree and varnished it and put it backstage where the performers approach the stage. It's all shiny from where people have rubbed their hands on it for good luck.

Getting back to 'Sliding Through Life on Charm', I knew this
was a great title. I've had it in my head for twenty years. It
started off as fun, like these ideas do. Then I succumbed to one
of my faults. I got hung up on the rhyme and, of course, that
was a mistake. There are five or maybe six rhymes for 'charm'
in English: 'arm', 'alarm', 'farm', 'calm', 'marm' and 'smarm'.
These are not the makings of a rock and roll song. So
twenty-two years later, or maybe eighteen years later, I was in
despair. I was flipping. I knew it was still a great title. I
thought, now who can I get to write it? My eyes lit upon the
young Jarvis Cocker, who is an amazing lyric writer – just
amazing.

Jarvis was walking one way as I was walking the other way in a
TV studio. I knew he'd been to my shows, and I've been to his,
and, as we crossed paths, I just grabbed him and said, 'Jarvis, if
I give you a title, can you write the song?' He's very laconic.
'Maybe,' he said. I looked him straight in the eyes and said, very
slowly and very clearly, 'Sliding Through Life on Charm'. I
could see something happening in his eyes. He does look Robert
Mitchum-like in a very skinny way. He said, 'Well, yeah. Any
other information?' I said, 'No.' We moved on. He said, 'I'll
try.'

Three years later, I got a package in the mail in Dublin, and it
was the demo of 'Sliding Through Life on Charm' and the
lyrics scribbled in pencil on the back of an envelope. At first, I
couldn't quite understand them. Only when we recorded it did
he tell me what he did. He read my book. He took the theme
out of that book. He told me that reading it had been an

absolute revelation, and he didn't get it wrong. He decided to stand up for me. What amazed me – and I've noticed this with these great, great people, especially these young ones – they can look into your soul. And what he did was say what I really think but was too afraid to say. Because after the Stones' drug bust at Redlands, I was fucking terrified. I've never really recovered. To this day I am too scared to move back to England.

The chainsaw sound at the beginning of 'Sliding Through Life on Charm' is a metaphor, we're not actually into power tool orchestrations. It's not a real tree, of course, it's a family tree that's being cut down. 'The family tree was chainsawed Wednesday week.' What's interesting is that Jarvis thought I came from a very grand family with a lot of money. Not true about the lots-of-money bit, of course, but on my mother's side, it is quite grand. Back to Charlemagne, eight hundred years. And on my father's side, there's the wonderful, nutty Faithfulls – missionaries and teachers and professors of Renaissance studies as well as sexologists running off with circus dancers. I don't really know what his words mean . . . yet I do. I just love 'em. That thing about, 'Go ahead, why don't you leave me to these thugs and creeps who want to fuck a nun on drugs?' He just nailed it. Great spiky lines – 'I had to know how far was going too far' and 'I wonder why the schools don't teach anything useful nowadays, like how to fall from grace and slide with elegance from a pedestal I never asked to be on in the first place.' Nobody else could have written that – I just gave him the title and he was off. Jarvis is sort of *like* his lyrics: whimsical, funny, wry.

Then we come to a lovely little David Courts/Marianne song. 'Love and Money' was written two years ago. Dave wrote the music, and I wrote the lyrics. But in a songwriting partnership you can't just blithely say, 'I did everything on this level, and he did everything on that level.' You really can't. It's always fifty-fifty. David isn't a professional musician, a muso; it's his hobby. He doesn't write for anybody else. I like that.

We wanted it to sound like it came from another era, so Dave and I and David Boyd, who ran my record company at the time, took it down to Chris Potter, who is one of the great engineers/producers/mixers of all time, and mixed it for nothing on Rolling Stones' recording time. He gave it that retro sound, as if it had been lying in a vault since 1967.

'Nobody's Fault' is, as you may know, a Beck original from his album, *Mutations*, and the minute I heard it, I started jumping up and down, saying, 'That's mine! That's mine!' Oh, and that's real musicians playing in real time on 'Nobody's Fault' I want you to know.

I knew Beck well enough to know that if I could catch him I might be able to really grab his interest, but I was ready for a 'no' and able to take it. And I did get Beck to write another song especially for the album. We agreed to meet at the Olive Garden in Venice, California. While I was waiting for him to arrive I was sitting there, staring at the ducks, holding my notebook, thinking, I've got a genius arriving in an hour and I haven't got anything written. I quickly went through my notes of the last two years and knocked out a final version of 'Sex with Strangers', which had been cooking away quietly for a while. I took a lot of the images from *Intimacy*, the Patrice Chéreau film I was in. It's all about sex with strangers. So that's where it comes from. It's not personal experience (I hate to disappoint you). It's not actually about Beck or me having sex with strangers. It's just a construct. But a sexy one.

I'm as fascinated as anyone by other people's sex lives, but my own sex life I insist on keeping private. I know from my gay friends quite a bit about sex with strangers, though personally I prefer sex with my friends. I always have. But can I imagine it? Easily!

Having sex with strangers is generally more of a male fantasy, but in my song, it isn't. The way I did it at the Barbican Centre in March 2002 was in a raincoat with a hat and a cigarette and leaning against a lamppost. It wasn't any male fantasy, I can tell you.

Another thing that people don't realise – the incredible generosity of musicians to each other. They didn't need to do all this stuff for me – and for nothing. They're all superstars in the middle of huge careers, particularly Damon. There I'd be, behaving as usual, and Damon would be waiting two hours for me to arrive at the studio. Sorry, Damon!

It was so curious working with these musicians all quite a bit younger than myself. Beck, Blur, Billy Corgan, Pulp. The thing about teen rock stars, as far as I know the species from the boys – they're not boys, of course, they're young men – is that they are a very interesting generation to work with. They've gone through the early bit where they think they're God. They were all at very interesting points of their own lives. Crossroads. I was very careful in how I approached them. I would never hustle people. Strike that. If they didn't want to do it or didn't have the time, I would have just dropped it, but they all had a moment and wanted to. Some of them must have enjoyed it because a couple of weeks after it came out I got an e-mail from Billy saying, 'When do we start on the next record?'

my life as a magpie
(an annotated faithfullography)

Ah, yes, my proliferating film career. I've played God (twice in *Ab Fab*), I've played the Devil (Pegleg in *The Black Rider*), I've played Marie Antoinette's mother (*Marie Antoinette*), a professional wanker (*Irina Palm*), a club singer (*Crimetime*), a mother (*Moondance*), a Bev in *Shopping*, a Lilly in *When Pigs Fly*, a Betty in *Intimacy*, a Helen in *Far from China*, and a Pink Floydish mum in *The Wall: Live in Berlin*. Not to mention various appearances of my disembodied voice such as the Narrator in *The Turn of the Screw*. And of course I do have the dubious distinction, back in the day (1967), of being the first person to say 'fuck!' in a major motion picture – *I'll Never Forget What's'isname* with Orson Welles.

One of the reasons I like making films is that they allow me to be an amateur again. I never went to drama school, I've had to learn as I went along, but I hardly consider myself a professional. I would never want to be too professional – not that there's much chance of that! – I just bang on. I've always rationalised that professionalism is a particularly male thing. Women, unless they're complete puppets, have a harder time doing that – we're different – at least I am. I have to go out there and then come back and recover, because it takes so much out of you. Of course I do admire all that driven-ness and naked ambition. Madonna and Britney, et al. And I have no desire to resolve any of my ambivalence.

In 2004 I played Pegleg – the Devil – in *The Black Rider,* a play with a text by William Burroughs, music by Tom Waits, and directed by Bob Wilson. What more could you want? I was excited and delighted to get the part. It was the opportunity of a lifetime, but, of course, most people, especially of my age and medical history, don't do three months' stage work and then go straight out on tour. That's where I ran into trouble.

The play hangs on a magic silver bullet. A very Burroughsian concept. He chose to centre his text around the one traumatic event that affected his whole life – his William Tell act when he accidentally killed his wife Joan in Mexico City in 1951 during a drunken party. Joan balanced a glass on her head; Burroughs's shot hit her in the forehead, killing her. As he seems to imply in *The Black Rider*, the rest of his life would be an atonement for this desperate act. Burroughs is saying, This is what happened. That's how I read it. And the play and Joan's death are inextricably connected, since, as he has often said, 'I am forced to the appalling conclusion that I would never have become a writer but for Joan's death.'

The protagonist makes a deal with the Devil. Put down the pen, pick up the gun.

The bullet may have its own will
You never know who it will kill

These are very eerie lines. He aims at a bird, but he kills his lover; the bird he kills is his sweetheart, who is found dead. It's an irony that this terrible incident both began Burroughs's writing career and was the last thing he ever wrote about.

When I saw a production of *The Black Rider* in Hamburg, Pegleg was played by a man. We don't know if the Devil is a man or a woman, but it was an odd choice to use a woman. According to some sources, Eve had an intimate relationship with the Devil, but I don't buy any of that. That's just patriarchal shit.

I made my Devil rather charming, I thought. I wore white make-up and a strange straight mouth, not my mouth at all, and I wore a black wig. I didn't look anything like myself. I also wore an evening dress with two *very* long tails, like a tail coat, that went on and on and on.

I open the play. I come out and sing, playing it rather lighter. Everybody in the play is under the Devil's control, my control. The Devil is the *deus ex machina*. None of the characters is real until I animate them. They each come out of a wardrobe as some sort of puppet. It's a strange production, all intensely noirish, with German Expressionist colours and shapes. Very Robert Wilsony, in fact.

I found it hard work, very difficult, but I had the most wonderful time when we were playing in San Francisco. Francis Ford Coppola and his wife Eleanor came to the show – which is how my friendship with Sofia and the Coppolas began, leading eventually to my part in *Marie Antoinette*.

The first important part of my acting career came with *Intimacy*, the Patrice Chéreau film in which I played a working-class woman called Betty. I based my character on Kate Moss's mum, Linda, Croydon accent and all. I had a voice coach and everything, but her character, her type, was based on Linda.

Intimacy is about sex with strangers, which is where I got the idea for the song I wrote with Beck on *Kissin' Time*. One of the loveliest things about *Intimacy* is the quite graphic nude scenes. They look like Lucian Freud paintings. Those pale bodies, just the mounds of flesh, warts and all type of thing. Patrice says he didn't do it consciously, but on the other hand, directors are very cunning. Many directors use painters as their palette for the tone of their movies – whether they want the look to be lit dramatically and contrasty, like a Caravaggio, or soft moody browns like a Rembrandt. In any case the sex scenes have the tone and vibe of Lucian Freud nudes – neither are specimens of the race and both have that beautiful blue-tinted skin which Lucian finds very attractive.

The last day of shooting was the hardest. Claire, the woman involved in the affair, has been mean to my character so Kerry

Fox and I had to act out a row. Patrice, being a perfectionist, did take after take, some wide shots, then cutting to Kerry for close-ups, etc. When I got back I wanted to kill myself – I had convinced myself that I was a complete amateur who would never do anything good. And François passed out on the bed. I was really upset because I really needed someone to talk to.

When Patrice screened a clip of the film he had put together for Cannes at a party at his apartment, I realised that the star of the film was London. It's not shot in those parts of London that you'd expect but places like Blackheath and New Cross. The scene with Kerry Fox and me walking and talking on Clapham Common in the dawn looks so beautiful, but I was a bit unnerved at my appearance – it's utterly un-glamorous – I'm just an ordinary woman who takes drama classes. I have no make-up on and I'm dressed in a funny way – so it was a bit of a shock to see myself on the screen like that.

Intimacy had the misfortune to open in the United States on 9/11. God, what bad luck! So it never really got a chance, but it's a wonderfully disturbing film.

Then came my first starring role, as Irina Palm in Sam Garbarski's film of the same name. There are some really funny scenes. It's a study of the mixture between the beautiful and the grotesque. But not for one minute do you see Maggie as Marianne Faithfull. And, of course, I love it so much, because there's nothing I like better than being someone else! It was my idea to dye my hair brown. Maggie couldn't be a blonde. She has her own kind of beauty as a character, but it's not sexual. Nobody will ever get me to wear clothes like that again except in a picture! I had huge qualms about playing this part at the beginning, but I followed Roman Polanski's advice: know your lines and stay straight and just do it – and don't *act*. And it worked.

I have far less anxiety about acting in films than I do about performing. But that's because I'm acting, playing somebody else. Anyway, I think good actors always have a streak of insecurity in them, which is to their advantage because it's that subtext of anxiety that makes a performance compelling. One of the most awful things is an actor who is completely sure of himself. Good actors are fluid, and that flicker of worry and insecurity intensifies their performance.

———————————

My favourite part so far has been Maria Teresa in Sofia Coppola's *Marie Antoinette*. I used my mother as the model for the aristocratic mother of the doomed queen. Before filming began I'd had bronchitis twice, very badly, and that's why I got so overweight – because I had to take cortisone. Dear Sofia didn't say that, she's too nice, but I couldn't stop myself from saying, 'Oh God, Sofia! I'm worried I'm going to be *so fat*!'

'Well, Marianne,' she said, 'you are rather *buxom*, but don't worry, it'll work as *period* buxom,' which was, I thought, very gracious – and, indeed, it won't matter since Maria Teresa, the historical character, had twelve children, so she certainly wasn't thin!

In a way *Marie Antoinette* is not that much different from *Lost in Translation*. It's more elaborate and frenetic, of course – it's all about decadence, but at its centre there's the character of the young girl trying to come to terms with the life she's in, which all Sofia's films so far have been about. This one just happens to be the Queen of France. It's as if Kate Moss were the Queen and Pete Doherty were Louis XVI. As Maria Teresa says of her in the film: 'People of France, I'm sending you an angel,' but essentially she was sold into slavery. My impression of the movie: sexy candy, pop daydream confections with sherbet colours and American accents.

Sofia is Hollywood royalty. She was groomed from an early age to fulfil her role; at twelve Francis was discussing second-act problems with her. Sofia Coppola's note to me about my character was: 'Be more cool, be more strong; think of your mother. You're a great empress, be intimidating, imposing, but with warmth.'

The great thing about the Coppolas is that they're a real Italian family. It's such fun hanging out with them. At lunch I sat near Roman. He was telling me about Walter Salles, the guy who did *The Motorcycle Diaries*, the Che Guevara movie. He's a friend of Roman's and he's making a movie of Jack Kerouac's *On the Road*. It's a project Roman and Francis have been interested in for a long, long time, with Francis producing. Walter Salles is coming over to Paris to talk to me about Allen

Ginsberg, Gregory Corso, and Bill Burroughs. And I did manage to say to Roman, 'Well, actually, Carolyn Cassady, Neal Cassady's wife, is still alive. Also, there's Joyce Johnson.' 'Well, I know,' Roman said, 'but we didn't want to make a film that's only from the girlfriend's or the wife's perspective, like *Bird,* the Charlie Parker movie, you know? There's a lot of films like that.'

But I had plans for my participation in this film other than in an advisory capacity. I hope I can play a librarian or something. I can't think of any other part I could play.

'Couldn't I just play a lady working in a diner?' I asked Roman.

'Not really. You don't really *look* like a lady who works in a diner.'

'Well, but I could be some character on the road! I'd probably be better in a bar. Some mysterious old broad in a bar. I'd love that! I could be a Salvation Army sergeant and convert Kerouac and Cassady.'

'We'll see,' he said.

I can see what my role is going to be in the next ten years; I'm going to be called for parts involving eccentric old broads.

I went to Cannes with the intention of not drinking, but you can't get through the Cannes Film Festival without the odd glass of champagne. And going to lunch with the Coppola family you can't exactly refuse when Francis Ford Coppola says, 'You must try this wine.'

But it's possible that I put a bit of pressure on my kidneys there and I got very stressed out, because the second day after I got back to Paris I had terrible pains, and that night I was in hospital. It was not exactly helped by stress, champagne, and more glasses of wine than I normally drink, let's put it like that.

I came back from nearly dying only to find out that the most successful film in Paris at that moment was *Marie Antoinette*! At Cannes, they had booed. But what do they know in Cannes? Winning prizes and stuff like that is only important if *you* win. But I can't remember doing something that people liked that much for a long, long time.

————————

I have a small part in Gus Van Sant's sequence in *Paris, je t'aime*. All these different directors – the Coen Brothers, Wes Craven, Walter Salles, Gus and so on – tell the story of a romantic encounter in an *arrondissement* of Paris. Gus picked the Marais, which is the gay area of Paris but also one of the most beautiful districts. It's the old Jewish area, and also where Patrice Chéreau lives.

————————

Sometimes even the benign images of me are misguided, as I learnt when I did an ad for Virgin Atlantic in 2000. It was shot at Shepperton; filmed in this huge hangar where they make the James Bond and *Star Wars* movies. I was cast in the commercial as a glamorous rock star moll – strange because the point of this series of ads was that we were meant to represent ourselves. The gist of the script they gave me went something like 'I've been in more limousines than the president.' My first reaction was, 'I *have*?' Limousines, for heaven's sake! My life hasn't been like that at all! That sort of thing was only starting to happen when I stopped hanging out with the Stones. I tried to explain this to the director, but it quickly dawned on me that their idea of decadence and mine are worlds apart. It took me a minute or two to realise that one doesn't argue with advertising people – especially if one is getting well paid for twelve hours' work.

After I made *Girl on a Motorcycle* in 1968 I used to get a lot of 'Dear Miss Faithfull . . .' letters from young boys who went into ecstatic reveries about the solitary pleasure I'd given them in my skin-tight leather jumpsuit. The plot was elementary and a bit nutty.

Of course I couldn't ride a motorbike at all. I was on a trolley with a wind machine, shot against a blue background. It's a riot because the film swings between endless shots of me on a motorcycle with the wind blowing my hair, stripped-in scenery, and Rebecca's stream-of-consciousness silliness. It's kind of Existentialism on a motorcycle with trippy polarised flashbacks. He was a good director, old Jack Cardiff, great shots – Jack was principally a cinematographer so the look of the film is great. I remember thinking that it looked like a sort of glorified Harley Davidson ad. I was too young and too self-conscious to be able to be aware of any of it, really, but I'm very pleased that I made a film at the age I did, because it preserved me in aspic at one of the periods of my life when I looked really good. I'm doing my best, anyway.

mind movies

Before the Poison – a slightly prophetic title, I think!

The child on the cover represents the question the album asks. She's the future. What will happen to this child? What kind of world will she find when she grows up?

'Mystery of Love', that's very much Polly – the brilliant, prolific, shape-shifting singer-songwriter P. J. Harvey. It's about the unnerving vortex of love, longing, and doubt. An inseparable dance of emotions as love passes through anxious suspensions and unsettling questions. It's an uptempo number, but hard to do night after night, so I tend not to sing it on tour. The next cut, 'My Friends Have', Polly just came out with one night after we'd finished working. She knows all my friends: Chris Blackwell, Paul and Cathy McGuinness, Carrie Fisher, David and Coco Dalton. With friends like that I can go anywhere, live anywhere and Polly decided to write a song about that.

My friends have always been there,
To help me shape my crooked features
My friends have picked me up again,
And pushed my enemies out of the picture

It has a kind of Kinks-ish quality to it – a song about anything can be anything. Polly plays guitar on it, she's got this fantastic style that's a bit like drumming. Barry Reynolds does it too; a very percussive rhythm.

So we have Polly on guitar on her song, and, next up, Nick Cave on piano on the song I wrote with him: 'Crazy Love'. The way I'd planned the album was for everyone to pick a movie and use that movie as the theme for the song we'd write. Polly and I, for instance, picked Louis Malle's *Pretty Baby* for 'Mystery of Love'. Nick Cave wasn't that interested in my movie idea, but I followed it anyway. 'Crazy Love' I based on the classic old French film, *Les Enfants du Paradis*. When I was writing the lyrics to 'Crazy Love' I got stuck because I couldn't find my copy of the DVD, so François proceeded to act out the entire movie for me, scene by scene. He's got the most amazing memory. He became my own walking, talking *Les Enfants du Paradis*.

The villain in the film is Pierre-François Lacenaire, the really evil one, seething with cynicism ('The mere thought of them killing each other over a woman because of me comforts me'), the one who kills the rich businessman in the end.

Hated by all and everywhere he goes
Blazing contempt for human life and lies
Murder as art and what he knows he knows
From life and fear in other people's eyes

And then Arletty:

She walks the boulevard without a care
Knowing too much but having come so far
Pretending life is just a game you play for nothing
Loving no one and nowhere

These two opposites are mirrored in the music. Nick plays a falling piano and the voice goes up.

And then we come to 'Last Song'. This was a song that Damon wrote at the end of the *Kissin' Time* sessions. The music is his, some of the words are his, some are mine. There was a bit of drama about it because at first he didn't want to let me have it. He'd forgotten he'd written it and, when he remembered, he realised what a great song it was.

It's deeply ironic. The lines

We saw the green fields
turn into homes
such lonely homes

are a lament for the last of England, the end of England, the loss of the green fields which have been its glory – Blake's 'green and pleasant land' turned into subdivisions. With the new housing developments going up everywhere you can forget about Blake's Countenance Divine shining forth upon our clouded hills.

'No Child of Mine' is another Polly song. Journey of the mother to the son, which naturally I identify with, considering my somewhat fraught relationship with my son Nicholas. So for me its meaning fluctuates, depending on how we're getting along. When Nicholas and I had our last big row, it meant one thing, now it means something else. I've changed the lyrics slightly.

Songs tend to change their meanings as the years go on. And one of the most amazing ones for that is 'Broken English'. On the record I sing, 'What are you fighting for?' But when I sing it now on tour I say, 'What are *we* fighting for?' The world has changed, so the lyrics change.

The song 'Before the Poison' comes from a news item about a poison gas attack in the Tokyo subway by the Aum Shinrikyo doomsday cult in 1995. Sarin gas. I was imagining what it would feel like to have been there.

'There is a Ghost' is about all the people all over the world who have been killed. It started out as 'The Disappeared', which is what the Irish call the people killed in the Troubles, and the Argentinian mothers call their sons murdered by the death squads. I just took it further. My ghost is the symbol of all the ghosts. All the people who have been shot and thrown into pits.

In particular those people murdered due to ethnic cleansing in the Balkans, in Africa. The missing. That is their plaintive cry:

When you remember who I am
Just call

'Desperanto' is a black pun on Esperanto, the universal language created in 1887 by L. L. Zamenhof. The word 'esperanto' means 'one who hopes', but in my song it's desperanto, a language of despair.

Desperanto spoken here,
Today I hear it everywhere,
It is the language of Despair
It's in your nails and it's in your hair
It's in your mouth instead of air
It's in your house
It's in your heart
It's in your mind
It's everywhere
Today I hear it everywhere
It's in your tiny little prayer

Well, there's a little gleam of hope at the end.

When I began to write 'City of Quartz', I based it on the classic movie, *The Third Man*. The evil of expediency, of greed and arrogance. That great speech where Harry Lime, looking down on a crowd from a great height, says: 'Would you really feel any pity if one of those dots stopped moving forever? If I offered you twenty thousand pounds for every dot that stopped, would you really, old man, tell me to keep my money, or would you calculate how many dots you could afford to spare?'

It began as that Orson Welles character, but then it went off into another direction, as these things often do. Once you give a song life you can no longer control it, and so the Orson Welles character in *The Third Man* morphed into L. Ron Hubbard. It's power-mad, money-mad people who see human beings as just things to be used.

I wrote 'City of Quartz' with Jon Brion, whom I'd met while I was working with Beck. Jon is an amazing singer-songwriter, producer, composer and Shiva-armed instrumentalist. I made a mental note to myself: Write a song with this guy; he's a genius! And he's actually a great record producer, too. He works with Fiona Apple and people like that. I didn't want a lot from him. I just wanted one song – a one-night stand. It's the last song on the record.

the girl factory

This is a long story about a short song, but the subject was so
odd and interesting I thought I'd tell it anyway. It introduced
me to the mysterious mind of Frank Wedekind, the German
proto-Expressionist playwright, notorious for his perversely
erotic dramas and gothic tales. His provocative cycle of Lulu
plays were made into the famous opera of the same name by
Alban Berg, and in his fiendishly clever play *Franziskaza* a
young girl sells her soul to the Devil in order to experience
what it's like to be a man.

When I was in Milan last year I had dinner with Roberto
Calasso, the Italian writer and publisher whose amazing books
I adore. It's hard to describe them because they are like the
Ganges, writing in which everything under the sun mixes and
fuses. Proust, Vedic hymns, Freud, Psellus on demons, Kafka,
Apuleius, Talleyrand, Gottfried Benn, Shiva, Marx's 18th
Brumaire, and Plato's myth of Er all engage in a fantastic
dialogue with his own multiphrenic intelligence. And although

The Marriage of Cadmus and Harmony and *Ka: Stories of the Mind and Gods of India* are works of stunning erudition, he rightly considers them novels – because that's what they are: ideas transmuted into cerebral poetics, all the great thoughts that any addled mind has pondered linked through his alchemical imagination in a great web of images and ideas.

He's an archaeologist of myths, and even over lunch, Roberto's ferocious polemical intelligence is awake, scanning everything you tell him and relating it to some subterranean stream. When I described my childhood at Braziers, Roberto paused momentarily.

'You know,' he said, 'it reminds me of a very strange story by Wedekind, one of his more enigmatic tales and a story which has particularly haunted me.'

'Oh, I love Wedekind,' I said, a little disingenuously, desperately searching my brain for some book or play I associated with the name. 'What's it called?'

'*Mine-Haha*, like the Indian princess in the Longfellow poem. Wedekind wrote it while imprisoned in the fortress of Königstein for writing a satire about Kaiser Wilhelm II's journey to Palestine. It tells the story of a vast girls' school in a Kafkaesque castle ... They're brought up in an isolated, secretive world. Nobody knows what goes on there. The narrator, now an old lady, was once a little girl there. The townspeople leave unwanted children – only girl children – by the castle gates, and these little girls disappear inside for sixteen years. The girls know nothing of life outside the castle's high walls. At the castle they're taught beauty, carriage, ballet, music, posture, elocution, how to please in general . . .'

'Not *exactly* my experience at Braziers, I suppose, but I do see some similarities,' I joked.

'Then,' he continued somewhat ominously, 'when the girls are sixteen they are thrown out into show business or become prostitutes or courtesans – sort of a geisha finishing school where they are brought up to please others. They're all interchangeable: if one disappears, another one can take her place – they're there to be *used* as delectable treats for the prince and his lusty courtiers.'

'But, of course,' I said, 'there's a *huge* difference between me and the girls in *Mine-Haha*, because nobody *forced* me to go to London and become a pop singer. *Tempted me*, definitely, *seduced* me into it, but I wasn't actually *compelled* to become a pop singer, whereas the girls in this castle are made to become performers with whips and torture.'

'Still,' said Roberto, 'perhaps your ability to survive so well in the sixties came from having grown up at Braziers as a child in a communal, utopia-seeking community.'

'Yes, of course, I know I *seemed* to fit in perfectly with the new mutant age, but at the same time my need to run away from it also came from Braziers. I was wary of its consequences – and, as it turned out, I became a prime example of the consequences.'

'I find it interesting that you grew up in a similarly cloistered place to the castle in the Wedekind story, and that at seventeen, you, the same age as those girls, burst out into the world, trained, in a strange way, for all sorts of things – group politics, sex, books, dance, acting, singing – that were useful to you in your career.'

'Well, it's true I was taught all sorts of things that I was able to use in pop music and that also had parallels to the sixties obsession with communes, the collective unconscious spilling itself all over the streets. I can see how even the group mind concept my father taught at Braziers must have helped me a lot in fitting in. Probably why I fitted in so easily with the Stones. They were like a little tribe, you know, a rock'n'roll gang. I had no problem adapting to that, but in the end it was at the cost of my own ego.'

'But, what fascinates me, though, are the *affinities* between Braziers and *Mine-Haha*, the mixture of isolation and eroticism, education and entertainment. Don't you find that odd?'

'I had such a strange upbringing at Braziers . . . and that, combined with the sexually charged nature of the place – my grandfather and his nutty sexological theories, and everybody there shagging night and day – there are certainly overtones of *Mine-Haha* there. I'm just glad I wasn't one of those girls . . .'

Mine-Haha is so perversely erotic and freaky and anti-society, and that's probably why it's never been translated into English. It's too weird. Before the girls are sent out into the world they're examined from head to toe, internally, externally, the whole thing. It's really perverse. Anyway, none of that happened to me, obviously.

Oddly enough, there have been two movies made of Wedekind's story: John Irvin's slick, soft-core *The Fine Art of Love: Mine Ha-Ha* and Lucile Hadzihalilovic's mysterious *Innocence* with its hothouse atmosphere. The Italian dance troupe, Gruppo Polline, picked up on the disturbing and suggestive undercurrents of *Mine-Haha* out of which they created a cultural-political-feminist performance piece. They describe its themes as: 'The persistence of memory, isolation, the hesitation about the future, alternating static and frenetic, and the negation of body as a result of an education based on theories and exploitation of the young.'

Mine-Haha is a fairy tale that morphs into something far more grotesque – a psycho-sexual Expressionist fable. And although my upbringing at Braziers and *Mine-Haha* are not exactly analogous, it was one of Roberto's essays, 'Déesses entretenues' ('Kept Goddesses') in his book, *The Forty-Nine Steps*, which inspired me to write 'In the Factory' with Polly Harvey. I was going to call it 'The Girl Factory' but Polly wanted it to be a bit more mysterious. I now wish I'd stuck up for myself. I do love Polly so much, but she's quite intimidating.

Every song is a self-portrait, in a way, but you don't really want to feel like, Oh, I'm sitting down to write another fucking song about myself!

a lean and hungry hook

Writing songs on demand for other people's projects I find quite a bit trickier than working on my own material. At one point I was asked to write lyrics to a tune for a French gangster film, based on the first half of *Julius Caesar*. They sent me some music that didn't do anything for me and wanted me to write the lyrics, but I couldn't think of *anything*. Total blank.

Then François called me in Africa where I was staying to remind me about it and I panicked. No way, I can't do it until I get back, I said. But then I found a copy of Shakespeare in the house – you can count on finding Shakespeare and the Bible almost anywhere – and I took a look at *Julius Caesar* again and, blah-di-blah-blah, I suddenly realised that I'd got a lot of it in my head. I'd remembered it; it all came rushing back. Under the influence of Shakespeare's heady blank verse I wrote it pretty much there and then on the spot, the spot being Lamu, an island off the coast of Kenya. Once I got the line I was off and running, I was fine. It's called 'A Lean and Hungry Look'. Of course, we know 'Yon' Cassius has a lean and hungry look,' but, other than that, I avoided any direct quotations from the

Bard; there's no Ides of March or *et tu, Brute*. Still, you'd have to know Shakespeare pretty well to fluff it. When I got back the movie people came round and they absolutely loved it. Oh well, another panic attack for nothing! Unless of course you put it down to the panic attack leading to the creative burst. Scary, though. I was so relieved when they said they didn't want to change a word. Collaboration is great, but not changing a word is better.

juliette gréco

When I was a young girl, Juliette Gréco was my absolute idol.
She was the ultimate bohemian Existential girl. There's a
photograph of her waking up in her Saint-Germain-des-Prés
flat at three o'clock in the afternoon. Bottles of wine,
newspapers and books are strewn on the floor; she's smoking a
Gauloise, and putting some Stan Getz on her little bedside
turntable. What more do you need to know? Her love affair
with Miles Davis was just perfect. She described him as 'A real
Giacometti with a face of great beauty.' Jean-Paul Sartre – as
Existential matchmaker! – asked Miles why they weren't
married.

'Because I love her too much to make her unhappy,' Miles
replied.

Of her, Sartre famously wrote that her voice 'encompasses
millions of poems'. Her life was a bohemian fairy tale played
out against a backdrop of ferocious intellectual debates between
Sartre and Camus at the Café de Flore, staying up till dawn in
the wild smoke-filled jazz dives and cabarets of the rue

Dauphine, hanging out with Dizzy Gillespie, Charlie Parker, Miles and Boris Vian, attending earnest political discussions about anarchy and the Spanish Civil War . . . Her face alone was a hieroglyphic for everything intense, hip, and cool in Paris's post-war bohemia.

Jean Cocteau saw her at the legendary club Le Tabou and cast her in a starring role in his film *Orphée*, poets vied to write lyrics to her songs – Louis Aragon, Jacques Prévert, Raymond Queneau – with Prévert writing her aptly self-descriptive classic, *'Je Suis Comme Je Suis'* ('I Am What I Am').'

When I first looked at pictures of her in magazines and on her record covers I would imagine her exotic life. Very intellectual, very political, very anarchist. As teenagers, she and her sister Charlotte joined the Resistance (along with their mother) and were imprisoned by the Gestapo. She was defiant and fearlessly political; one of her more rebellious acts was to perform a concert in Chile in 1981, then under Pinochet, to an audience of soldiers and generals, singing only anti-war, anti-fascist songs.

Despite her indelible personality she remains as mysterious as the Mona Lisa. Her lovers were poets, painters, philosophers, gangsters, jazz musicians, but nobody will ever know much about *her*. Her life was *insolite*, strange, elusive. She tapped into the mystique – and it's still there. François and I went to see her not long ago and she looks *just the same*. It's uncanny, really. That long black hair, like some curtain at the entrance to a fortune-teller's tent, is a national symbol of hipness, resistance, sensuality and mystery. She hasn't exactly led a puritanical life and she hasn't had plastic surgery either. Juliette doesn't look young, but she doesn't look at all weird or grotesque – she still looks like Juliette Gréco, beautiful and mysterious.

She nearly died recently, from a bad case of cancer, but she's back and on tour at eighty! Unstoppable and sphinx-like. Whenever I run into her she's always very gracious – I'm sure she can see that I worship the ground she walks on.

La Gréco! She's my role model for life. If I want to be anybody, I want to be Juliette Gréco. Have a love affair with Miles Davis and sing sublime Existential poetry the rest of your life. That's how you do it.

incident on boogie street

In 1974 Oliver Musker and I were staying at Raffles in
Singapore – the old Raffles Hotel – it's now quite ghastly, but
back then it still reeked of faded colonial splendour. Oliver is
the knight in shining armour who came and rescued me at my
darkest hour, swept me away from all my demons and off to
exotic locations. One evening Oliver and I decided to seek out
an opium den on Bugis Street, affectionately known as Boogie
Street, in the red-light district. We were both rather foolishly
dressed as if we'd just stepped out of *A Passage to India*.
Oliver in his white suit and panama hat, and I in a topi with
a veil and a long grey suit with grosgrain on the collar and
hem.

Unbelievably stupid to go down to Boogie Street looking like a
couple of twits from the British Raj. Darling Oliver, who really
is such a sweet guy. He eventually married an Indian girl and
now lives in India, so he's mellowed a lot, but in those days he
had an unfortunate habit of going, 'Come along now, chop
chop!' to natives who understandably did not take his
supercilious attitude too well. Suddenly we were surrounded by

a gang of thuggish Chinese felons and then I heard this terrifying sound – *swishhhhhhh-hhhh-eeeeee* – as they brought their knives out.

And I thought, 'Right, that's it! We're going to die – and in this incredibly stupid way!' And then out of the blue who should appear but Roderick O'Connor, younger son of a good Irish family, on his way to Australia to try to pick up an inheritance, which he did not manage to do (he subsequently went to India to do a bit of grave robbing). He's a chancer but a really good friend of mine. Brave, quick-witted Roderick just stepped into this situation and addressed these vicious thugs in Chinese – obviously telling them something like, 'Don't bother with these two; they're completely stupid' – and made them fall over laughing. He got rid of them just like that and we walked away.

Then Roderick took us to an opium den. It is the only opium den I've ever been to and it was as sublime as I'd always imagined it to be. A lot of people lying around on couches in deep dream states. You lay your head on a wooden pillow, servants prepare your opium pipe, and you fall into the most blissful reverie, for I

> *on honey-dew hath fed,*
> *And drunk the milk of Paradise.*

But, you know, even without Oliver's colonial condescension we might well have stirred up the Boogie-dwellers' wrath because we looked so mad. Of all the things to wear when you go to

Boogie Street! It's the sort of rough, criminal place you should go to wearing a leather jacket and jeans. And here we were, blithely ambling through Boogie Street's nightly transgender sex bazaar of 'Billy boys', freaks, drug thugs, and cutthroats, dressed up like Algernon Montcrief and Cecily Cardew in a revival of *The Importance of Being Earnest*. We *were* mad, mad in the way of characters who wander into the wrong movie, forget their lines and lose their lives.

bono busking

A few years ago John Boorman got me along to a press
conference in Stephens Green for Aung San Suu Kyi's fiftieth
birthday. She is the leader of the National League for
Democracy in Myanmar (formerly Burma), a devout Buddhist
and prisoner of conscience who defied the oppression of the
military junta. In 1991 she was awarded the Nobel Peace Prize
for her non-violent struggle against the repressive military
dictatorship.

She is unquestionably a noble and fearless heroine, but, no
matter how much I believe in a cause, sometimes it's hard
for me to even leave the house. But for John's sake and for
the very noble cause of San Suu Kyi's struggle I bestirred
myself. John directed a wonderful film about her, *Beyond
Rangoon,* a few years back and is very committed to her
case and to freedom in Burma. So although I was feeling
rather spaced out, I duly dressed up in one of my Jil Sander
suits and put on some make-up, and off I trotted, somehow
thinking Aung San would be there at the hotel to celebrate
her birthday! It was only when I got there that I realised that

the whole point of the thing was that she was under house arrest in Myanmar.

I walked in just as Bono was singing a song he'd written for her. I didn't at first realise it was Bono, although it did sound a bit familiar; I thought they had brought in one of the buskers from Grafton Street, you know how they all sound like him. Then I realised it *was* him and had a chuckle, imagining him with a hat on the ground, singing for a few coppers. Eventually, I posed for pictures with Bono and John Boorman for the cutting of the cake. John whispered in my ear, saying it was like the wedding we never had — which made me laugh so hard I practically fell *into* the cake.

m. st laurent's dog

I live now between Ireland and Paris – no culture shock there! It's hard to compare living in Ireland with living in France, because they're complementary, really. Paris is so chic and elegant and glamorous and dear old Dublin is a dirty old town.

In Ireland there's a lot of ragging, but here, since I don't speak French, I haven't a clue if people are putting me on or not.

I can't resist telling this apocryphal story about English and French ways of seeing things: there's an EU meeting in Brussels. The British propose a workable plan that everybody seems happy with. But then the French delegate takes the floor and says, 'Honourable members, this project is all very well in practice, but how will it work in theory?'

François, being French, is born ironic and he makes jokes that he has to then repeat and explain, because I don't really understand irony. When I'm watching a frightening film François has to come and comfort me because I get so scared. The other night I was watching *Gigi*, which I love because my mum took me to it as a child (and I love all the things I watched with Eva towards the end of her life, wonderful films like *Jean de Florette* and *Manon des Sources* and some of it is real crap like *Trapeze* but it doesn't matter). *Gigi*'s one of these films that make me cry and François, hearing me blubbering away, will come in to see if I am okay. After reassuring himself that I will survive this silly movie with Maurice Chevalier at his goofiest, he decides to go out, and as he's leaving he says to me, 'Are you sure you're going to be all right? Do call me if it gets too frightening for you!' Too frightening? Oh, I see, irony! *L'ironie en France*, cynicism in the UK. That more or less sums up attitudes to life across the Channel. Takes me a while, you see.

In England, sarcasm is the order of the day. It's not irony, it's toxic wit. It's cruelty, basically, and a very important part of English life, especially upper-class English life and intellectual English life, and it can be very funny as long as it doesn't come on you! I enjoy it tremendously. British cynicism and British sentimentality are two sides of the same coin actually. 'Sentimentality is the bank holiday of cynicism,' according to Oscar Wilde. Well, he means the over-ness of emotion that sometimes comes from people who are generally very cynical. When they do get emotional, they overdo it. Much like the death of Princess Diana, with the British getting all weepy and sappy about it.

Of course today, with the implicit cynicism about everything, ambivalence is in our DNA. Due to the culture, children at twelve are far more cynical than I probably will ever be.

Everything is ironic and camp to them. It's postmodernism or MTV or iPod commercials or fluoride in the water. And, you know, my generation never really had that.

French taste is something else – very different from the British. The English are essentially philistine, they consider exquisite taste foreign. I thought about this the other day when I dropped my keys as I was getting out of the elevator. They fell into the bottom of the lift shaft in Paris, and there was no way I could retrieve them. I have very nice neighbours upstairs, and they took me in and called somebody who got my keys back. And while I was there it was fascinating to see another version of our flat, but much fancier – all done in grey and gold.

I'm really very happy here in my friend's flat, just tucked up in Paris, being able to walk through this beautiful city. I went out the other night to get a breath of air and ran into Monsieur Saint-Laurent and his dog – a dear dog indeed. I love bulldogs – and Yves. These days it's getting difficult to tell them apart, actually. They're beginning to resemble each other in a startling way. Running into them sets off happy memories. Those wild, wonderful days we spent together in Morocco, getting high as kites and lounging on embroidered pillows.

my past attacks me (ned kelly)

Occasionally my past just sits up – in this case in the form of a famous toothy talking head – and hits me on the head.

In November 2000, I was having a wonderful time at the party *Vogue* threw at the Ritz. Lots of people I didn't know and a few I did. I chatted to Joely Richardson, who came up to say that she knew I had worked with her father Tony Richardson. We did *Hamlet*, and of course it was when I was going off to Australia with Mick to do *Ned Kelly* (which Tony also directed) that I took the Tuinol overdose (I was to play Ned's sister). I could never bring myself to see *Ned Kelly*. My part was taken over by a young Australian actress and that was that. A moment of shame. I'd always felt really bad about that, obviously – not a nice thing to do on someone's picture. So I said that to Joely – how I really fucked up on her dad's Ned Kelly film – but Joely was so sweet, saying, 'Oh come on, people do that all the time.' She told me to stop being so hard on myself about that incident (little does she know I'm not all *that* hard on myself). Still, what a dreadful thing to do on somebody's movie. What I should have said to myself back then was, 'I know what I'll do! I'll do this movie, and *then* I'll kill myself.'

looking roman polanski in the eye

The first time I met Roman Polanski was at Dr Tony's office. Tony was a script writer – a writer of pharmaceutical prescriptions, not of movie scripts – a doctor famous, in street parlance, for writing scripts for speed and downers. He was a good guy, Tony. It was Tony they called when Mama Cass choked on her ham sandwich – not much he could do about that – but he got a bad reputation as a Dr Feelgood, like all those other doctors who liberally dispense prescriptions to the needy (and deserving).

I was at Dr Tony's to get my prescription for sleeping pills, but I can't imagine why Roman was there – not being a druggie. Probably something to do with women. Tony being famous for giving out slimming medication, there were always *a lot* of very pretty girls in his office.

Soon Roman and I became friends. We'd go to the Ad Lib club together, smoke a joint and laugh. This was long before the Sharon Tate murders. Roman's way of handling depression is to work through it. Mine was to seek oblivion and sit on a wall.

One day Roman had a flash. 'Marianne, you must play Lady Macbeth in my film,' he said. And what do you say when Polanski asks you? You can't exactly say no, not me, anyway, because he's Roman. So I said, 'Of course, Roman, I'll do anything you like.' He had this great casting director at the time whom I liked very much called Maude Spector – she thought I could be a brilliant Lady Macbeth. Roman wanted me to do it, and I wanted to play the part more than anything. But there was one little problem . . .

Apart from that, it was as good as settled. I foolishly thought I could cover it up. I had to do a screen test, of course. I got up at five o'clock in the morning and the limo came and took me to Shepperton Studios where Roman was filming. At the studio there seemed to be *thousands* of people standing around. I got made up and came on set. Camera, speed, action! After about twenty seconds Roman shouted, 'CUT!' And from the tone of his voice I knew it was me. I knew I'd fucked up and I went into a tailspin. I wanted to say something but I was speechless. All I actually remember is a *really furious* little Roman practically stamping the ground like Rumpelstiltskin shrieking, 'What's the *matter* with your *eyes*?! WHY CAN'T YOUR EYES FOCUS?' I nearly died. But I just couldn't tell him, 'I'm having my own hard time, I'm on heroin!' The poor man couldn't understand what was the matter with me, why there was no life in my eyes. By noon I might have been okay, but at five in the morning I was still too doped up and out of it. I stood there frozen in shame and walked off with my head hung down. He couldn't understand how anyone could turn up like that when there was a job to do.

Too bad because I would've loved to play Lady Macbeth. I have that side, from my mother, probably. Dank *mittel-*European castles, millennial curses, black thoughts, and overweening ambition. Oh, I could have spoken with a vengeance those terrible lines with their consuming will to evil!

> *Come, you spirits*
> *That tend on mortal thoughts! unsex me here,*
> *And fill me from the crown to the toe top full*
> *Of direst cruelty; make thick my blood,*
> *Stop up the access and passage to remorse,*
> *That no compunctious visitings of nature*
> *Shake my fell purpose, nor keep peace between*
> *The effect and it!*

I had once played Ophelia on stage high on heroin – taking it just before the mad scene, it might even have helped in some perverse way. But Lady Macbeth is a different kettle of fish entirely. She demands steely resolve rather than willowy dementia; physically and psychically and in many other ways – spiritually, too, perhaps. I really wasn't capable of sustaining something like that. And, in any case, my performance wouldn't have been *intentional*. And it was a two-month shoot. I would have got to the three-week mark and conked out. Needless to say, I didn't get the part. It went to Francesca Annis. And I'm glad I didn't get the part, because the shape I was in, I would have screwed his movie up. And, fucking hell, did I have a tenuous grip on sanity then.

Wind forward to thirty-five years later. François and I go to see *Hedda Gabler*, with Roman directing his wife Emmanuelle Seigner in the role of Hedda. It was in French, but I know the play well enough it didn't really matter – I was a hippie Hedda Gabler myself. We went backstage and there was Roman with Emmanuelle. Emmanuelle, whom I'd met at the *Vogue* party, was charming and witty. But I was pretty scared of seeing Roman again actually. I knew I'd let him down very badly. And what are the first words out of Roman's mouth? 'What *was* the matter with your *eyes* that day?' He hadn't forgotten for a second! It was as if no time had passed. And so I explained it to him, 'Now look, Roman, you've *got* to understand. I *know* you were having a really hard time, but I was having my *own* hard time, self-induced it may have been, and, in addition to everything else, I was on *heroin*.' But, of course, he *doesn't* really understand. Drugs are not Roman's thing at all. Roman's way of dealing with trouble is work, work, work – and that's what he thinks everybody else should be doing, but it certainly wasn't what I was doing. And, of course, it's one of the greatest regrets of my life that I didn't work with Polanski.

The Irish playwright Frank McGuinness believes that *Macbeth* – the Scottish play, as we'd better start calling it – is in fact an actualisation of the Black Mass, and that explains – whether Roman knew it or not – *why* he was so drawn to it. It's a kind of exorcism.

I recently read Roman's memoir; it came out in 1982 originally, and unfortunately it stops just before his life began to improve so it ends on rather a downer. It's very honest and shows a far more vulnerable Roman than most people expect. At the very end I was fascinated to hear him say that people who don't know him think he's this poisonous dwarf. When I got to know him, I got a *completely* different picture of him. In person he's funny, light, and amiable. He delights in jokes and self-deprecating wit. As he says, 'I like shadows in movies. I don't like them in life.'

Like Bergman or Buñuel he's fascinated by the dark side, but he takes pains to separate his life from his films. His own experience has seen enough horror erupt catastrophically into his life, from his appalling childhood – the orphaned Polish kid (whose parents perished in a Nazi concentration camp) escaping from the Krakow ghetto, wandering through Europe in perpetual fear, and then the grisly Manson murder of his wife Sharon Tate and their unborn child. He's seen enough tragedy at first hand to want to distance his personal life from the chilling scenarios he conjures up on the screen.

The first sentence of his memoir reads, 'For as far back as I can remember, the line between fantasy and reality has been hopelessly blurred.' But there is nothing out of focus about his vision – he has a ferocious attention to details, the telling images that make his movies so unnerving. As I learned to my mortification, nothing escapes his ever-wary eye – or his crystal clear memory.

it was a good old wagon

The risk of a wrong decision is preferable to the terror of indecision.

MAIMONIDES, *Guide for the Perplexed*

Mad, mad days of life on the road. Bands, boozers, fuck-ups, scaly bookers, pernicious promoters, snarky journalists. Touring would be hard enough if all one had to do was get up and make a fool of oneself in front of thousands of people every night, but tours are also endless hassles. The hotels, the halls, the broom-cupboard dressing rooms. And we ought to mention a few other things that have happened that have been particularly barking.

No more sleeping under the van, though, thank God for that. That was when we were in a transit van going around Europe. We wrote *Broken English* in Berlin on that tour. Broke and English through the past darkly.

I don't leap about the stage like Sir Whatsisname, but even so, touring is physically demanding. Before going on the road I'm

like a race horse or a jockey or something, getting prepared.
I have to go into training. My sets usually run an hour,
seventy-eight minutes tops. I can't do great long gigs. I'm not
up for epic shows like Bruce Springsteen; mine are more like
little tableaux, but still it's hard on the old bod. Pilates is my
new system. It's all about weight and counterweight and a lot of
stretching. It doesn't involve big, bad, horrible, sweaty numbers,
which was never my style anyway. It's just an hour of strict
exercising and when you're rich and famous (I've somehow
managed to squeak into one of these categories) one of the
perks is that you can get somebody to come to the house and do
it for you. It's great for the areas of my body that get stressed
out – my neck and shoulders. And it's absolutely essential
psychological preparation, because as the day and hour approach
I begin to get the Fear. An oncoming tour is excitement and
fear all mixed up together. As I get physically stronger and go
out on the road I gain confidence. Another source of inspiration,
of course, is that one has to perform to make money to eat.
That's a wonderful spur!

On with the motley, the paint and the powder – and the
Christian Louboutin boots. To be exquisitely dressed is essential
paraphernalia for the Marianne Faithfull persona. Photographs
and fashion are the incestuous twins in the Fabulous Beast's
imaginary life. John Dunbar, my droll ex-husband, says that
shopping was my principal addiction before I discovered heroin.
He claims that I would go into a kind of shopping fugue state
in which I would buy masses of clothes that I would never wear
and never even bring home, as if they represented some sort of
psychic substance.

In my mad bowerbird sort of way I've always been prone to pick up beautiful glittering things. Shopping, as I've always said, is my form of Zen. I've befriended all the great frock-maker geniuses: Karl Lagerfeld, Marc Jacobs, John Galliano and, the youngest and hippest, Azzedine Alaïa. Beautiful red-soled boots by Christian Louboutin and two beautiful stage suits made by John Galliano – all this to create my stage creature – part fantasy, part mythology, part couturier-conjured illusion.

Last year I got to a perplexing point. Another one. Something was bothering me about how I was acting as a performer. I didn't understand what was going on and it frightened me. I felt I'd lost some of my ambition, at least that part of me that performs on stage. Something was missing and I was a little alarmed at what had taken its place. I love being on stage, I love performing, I love my work, but I no longer have that funny mixture of desire and dread I once had.

I always thought I wanted to become a professional, you know, like all the great divas, to go on stage with complete confidence – to make my life as a performer less fraught with anxiety. There's no real danger I'll ever become such a consummate professional that I'll get to the point where I'm actually *relaxed* on stage, but I am now no longer absolutely petrified before a performance. You are more in control, you know what you're doing (yeah right), you're less terrified (if only), but in all this you tend to forget the impulse that took you there in the first place. As you become more confident, what you're doing becomes this *other thing*. I found I wasn't enjoying it as much because the fear and joy are somehow connected. I think that's true of all art.

I've been thinking about that lately, in the sense that I don't want to lose my amateur status – not that there's any great danger there! I'll never be the cool, calm, collected chanteuse and I've come actually to enjoy the frisson of terror as the wuzzly little person quaking in the wings in her Christian Louboutin boots morphs into Marianne Faithfull.

According to Andrew Oldham – the Stones' sometime manager as well as my own – amateur jitters are my trademark. As in his 'The Four Stages of Marianne Performing':

1. When I first come on stage I look like I'm not meant to be there – the whole thing is a big mistake.
2. A look of terror comes over me, as if to say, 'What the fuck is this?!' Basically panic and more panic.
3. Then comes, 'God, I'm getting away with it!'
4. And finally, 'I *am* good, aren't I?'

Touring is a form of time travel, it brings back memories. You find yourself back in spots you played twenty, thirty years ago. It's not easy to think of Hull or Liverpool as examples of Proust's memory-inducing madeleine, but they can be, you know. On a tour of the North Country a few years ago I found myself having lunch in a little place down on the Liverpool docks. I remember my mother bringing me to these very docks when I was a little girl. I remember the ships and the men unloading them, the tall cranes and the rows of containers stamped with exotic place names like Zanzibar, Peru and Singapore. It was there my fascination with America began. I looked at the big liners and my mother said, 'This is where ships leave from . . . to go to the United States.' It's no longer a working shipyard like Hamburg. The old import and export buildings have been converted into restaurants, bars and knick-knack shops. I wonder what happened to all those people who worked here – the dock workers, the crews, the customs officials, the shipping clerks? But then, what happened to a lot of things?

The road is filled with ghosts. They pop up in the Alhambras and the Gaumonts. Old Brit rock'n'rollers from that pre-Beatles era in their gold lamé suits and their greased-back duck-tails: Billy Fury, Marty Wilde, and Joe Brown.

From my very early touring days I remembered the best fish and chip shops on earth are to be found in the North. Delicious fresh cod and chips all smothered with lashings of salt and vinegar, and let's not forget the mushy peas. Food that comes with its own specific gravity, that stings the lips and lies heavy in the stomach afterwards; wash it all down with cheap red lemonade or a warm can of Irn Bru and have a jolly good afternoon snooze.

———————

The lull of the road, the grind of the road and the occasional lapse when you let down your guard make touring so thorny. Performing can get you high and you have to be careful what you do with that energy. In New York a few years ago I made a big mistake after the gig. We were so high from the adrenaline (I did the show completely straight) that we went on to this club called the Lotus and joined a table with the Corrs and Bono and had a great old time. But I stayed up far too late talking and yelling over the loud music and woke up with *no voice*! Catastrophe and big drama because there was another gig that night. We called my pal Penny Arcade, who can fix anything you name, and she immediately called up this rock'n'roll doctor who administered a hefty dose of steroids . . . evidently this is the only thing that works if you have lost your voice through straining it. The doctor said he would only ever do this in an emergency – but it was either that or cancel the show.

I went on stage and explained to the audience about my voice: I said that I was going to attempt the gig but if my voice didn't hold out then I would have to stop the show and give everyone their money back. The first song was fucking awful – with my voice a distant, cracked, frog-like croak, but by the second number the pills began to work, my voice suddenly came back, and everything was all right.

Andrew Oldham came to the show. He'd flown in from Colombia, where he lives. I could no more live in South America than Antarctica. It would be a disaster. I had to laugh when Andrew told me he thought the speech about my voice had been a gimmick to give the gig a touch of suspense. So typical of Andrew, the über hustler.

There's the gig and then there's the après-gig. Backstage
behaviour is so peculiarly formal – it's almost like the protocol
at an embassy dinner. Extreme politeness, artificial bonhomie,
and given the awkwardness of the encounters no amount of
flattery is ever too much. 'You were brilliant, darling, *as always*!'
'Another *triumph* for La Marianne!' 'Your best performance
ever!' Ever? Still, I tend to believe it all. But when I find *myself*
doing it, laying it on with a trowel in the dressing room after
someone else's performance, it makes me wonder. I remember
going to see Ruby Wax's show at the Olympia in Dublin. It's a
wonderful old theatre and Ruby was very good – if not exactly my
cup of tea. Watching Ruby on stage I became overly impressed by
the very act of performance. How can someone stand up there
on stage for two hours and tell jokes? It wasn't even the content
of her show, it was more the fact that certain talented humans
had achieved this at all. Afterwards I trundled backstage and
went way over the top, complimenting her so excessively that
my voice began to sound shrill and false – hence insincere,
mocking, even, perhaps. Ruby with her red hair and blood-red
lips looked at me with disbelief. Was I putting her on? *Why*
was I putting her on? I made an especially odd exhibition of
myself considering that arch backstage interviewing of celebrities
– Imelda Marcos, Pamela Anderson – is her stock in trade.

The last show on that tour I got a note backstage immediately
after the gig from this guy called Ray who was in the Nashville
Teens back in the sixties. He gave me my first kiss when I was
twelve or thirteen. My father used to run these school camping
holidays at Braziers Park, and Ray was always there. He was
incredibly handsome, and he seemed a lot older than me back

then, but he could only have been fifteen or sixteen. He played guitar and had an Elvis look, a real working-class lad with oodles of charisma. He was a sweet guy, and after he kissed me I started to shake. I don't know why, but I think it was pure terror. So anyway, I got this note after the show saying, 'Marianne, you were just fantastic tonight . . . do you remember me?' And it just floored me! I remember when I was seventeen and touring, 'As Tears Go By' was in the Top Ten. Ray was also in the charts with the Nashville Teens. It was July or August of 1964 and his band had this huge hit with 'Tobacco Road'. I never met him again after that kiss, so to get this note out of the blue nearly forty years later just knocked me sideways and left me reeling. Of course I didn't dare go and meet him in the state I was in.

Well, touring is that wonderful hour and a half on stage, and soundcheck, which is always fun! But the rest of it is very difficult: in the airport, on the plane, in cinderblock dressing rooms, blah-di-blah-blah.

Stuff like cocaine and alcohol and shit like that just aren't an option any more. For me. I'm not putting it down; but in my band, nobody drinks, nobody smokes; they're bloody vegetarians. Touring is hard work at our age, but because we're healthy, we can do a three-month tour. You have to make a choice: are we going to work properly or just fuck around?

A tour goes much better when people are cool, and not on drugs and alcohol. And that's from my direct experience – I know whereof I speak. Because, you know, it's such hard work you don't have time and the human body, unless you're twenty, just can't take it. And then you've got to think of the future. Did it even occur to us when we were smoking and drinking and popping pills and snorting strange powders what toll it would take?

I once thought that growing up *meant* smoking and drinking. It looked so good, but I don't want to die from it.

I have to admit I can get a bit grand on tour – or anywhere else, for that matter – it's in my DNA, that's my excuse. Barry Reynolds, my long-suffering guitar player, tells the following story. I'm not saying it isn't true:

> That tour just Marianne and meself; one of our last gigs was the Town Hall in New York. And the gig was great. We got a fantastic review in the *New York Times*, everything was going well. Our last gig was in Baltimore and everyone was 'Ahh! It's over, we've done it!' Finally, you know.
>
> The plane takes off. Because she smokes, when Marianne gets on a plane she always sleeps, takes something and crashes out so she doesn't have to go through any kind of nicotine withdrawal.
>
> And, you know, Baltimore, it's, what, half an hour, or an hour flight. Anyway, Marianne's head is on my shoulder, she's completely out. Then we hit this storm and the plane starts going up and down. Everything's opening, luggage is falling out of the racks on the top. I mean, we really went through a serious storm.

Marianne was snoring through the whole thing. Eventually the pilot says, 'Ladies and gentlemen, I'm afraid we can't land in Baltimore because of the storm there, so we're going to have to divert the flight and land in Richmond, Virginia.' But even in Richmond, it was a very heavy landing. I was really nervous, I think everyone was, it was a bad situation all around, but Marianne slept through the whole thing.

We arrived and everyone just sat there in shock. We've just been through an hour of hell; there's luggage strewn all over the place. As soon as Marianne realises the plane has stopped, her eyes open and she turns round to me.

'What's going on?' she asks.

'Well, Marianne,' I explain to her, 'we're actually in Richmond, Virginia.' There is this pregnant silence after which she says, 'But, Barry, we're playing in Baltimore.' 'That's right,' I say, 'but we couldn't land there because there was this severe storm and so we had to land in Richmond.'

Five minutes elapse and Marianne turns around and says, as only Marianne can: 'Does the pilot realise we have a gig?'

———————————

I called my last tour 'Songs of Innocence and Experience', which had a nice, lyrical lilt to it, but then you get these very earnest people on the phone asking you in what way it relates to the early poems of William Blake. Little did they know I was secretly calling it 'Heartbreak House'.

Another aggravation on tour is the Stupid Needling Journalist, the sort who asks, 'How can you record "Working Class Hero" when you're not working class?' It's pathetic, I know, so pathetic that one barely knows how to react, but I'm very vulnerable – especially on the road – and never know what to say.

One of the things you have to avoid on the road is making yourself a target for the free-floating animosity that churns up in audiences. Dr Badwin, my psychiatrist, used to say, 'You must be really careful, Marianne, not to become a lightning rod for people's hatred.' An odd emotional equilibrium occurs: as much as you are loved, that much are you hated.

Before I go on stage, whoa! I've got better, but when I was young I used to throw up. A lot of people who have the kind of stage fright I have don't go on stage. It takes a hell of a lot to be able to get over that because there's nothing more terrifying than being on a stage when they don't like you. It's like death. All you can think about are the times you were on stage and they *hated* you, like that famous pork chop incident in Sligo.

sex, drugs and smoking

2004. One year I won't easily forget. Nor the next year, come to think of it. I came straight from playing the Devil in *The Black Rider,* the William Burroughs/Tom Waits opera, and went right into a promotional tour for my album *Before the Poison*, the record I'd written with Nick Cave, Polly Harvey, and John Bryan.

Pegleg had been my character's name and so, appropriately, I twisted my ankle a week into the tour. Most people don't do six months' stage work and then go straight out on tour; it was very unsettling. Even without the accident, I would've gone mad. I didn't know who I was, where I was, or *what* I was. I was still Pegleg, really. Okay, I guess the lack of time to decompress isn't that unusual: actors frequently go from film to film to film, but eventually they do go bonkers.

It wasn't long before I turned into a monster. Actually, I became the vocalist from hell before the tour even started – when I came back to Paris to rehearse. I don't know how the band coped – probably only because Barry Reynolds, my guitar player, and Fernando Saunders, my bass player, know me so well they've learned to do the water-off-a-duck's-back bit. But I definitely freaked out the keyboard player. And after I was done making everyone else crazy, I fell apart myself.

More or less clean, I went straight into five days of rehearsal, eight hours a day. I was exhausted, and the tour hadn't even *started* yet. And then, in Reykjavik, I was prancing about on stage, not in very high heels – that would've been death – but in short, beautiful Christian Louboutin boots. Hmm, I have a pair in black silk with gold bamboo on it and a slightly higher pair in snakeskin. And two beautiful suits made by John Galliano, one to be cleaned while the other is worn on stage. I'd much rather talk about them than my drug addiction! But where was I?

Oh, yes. Pegleg about to twist *both* ankles performing in Reykjavik. Falling in Christian Louboutin was getting to be a habit. I was hobbling, in agony. What I should have done was stay in bed for a week, but naturally it occurred to me that there were other options. My sympathetic record company was in agreement and said, 'Just take the pills and go on the road! Do what you've got to do to go on with the tour!' Big mistake. You've got to give the bloody crippled artist the week off. Now I must admit at the time the drug alternative was rather tempting. But something I now know for sure is that if there's one thing that does *not* have to go on, it's the show.

I was in terrible pain when I stood up, and I'm not one of those old blues singers who can sing sitting down. You should have seen me, on tour in a surgical boot. Black and blue up to the knee. I checked into a ridiculous hotel, one of those fancy modern places that are the most uncomfortable you can imagine – cramped, over-designed, furniture you're just meant to look at. Anita Pallenberg came to visit me and we fell about laughing. She is always great in dire situations.

With both Achilles tendons torn and swollen up to my thighs, I was in excruciating pain. I went to a doctor who prescribed painkillers. I neglected to tell him I'd been a drug addict. It just slipped my mind. Toplagique is what he prescribed. The moment I took one I felt *fantastic*. Not surprisingly, it turned out to be a morphine-based drug, and it didn't take long for the opiate demon to get its claws in me. I found out from my friend Pierre that when French junkies can't cop, they score Topalgique. I didn't need all that stuff, it was the record company pushing, saying I had to do the tour – so, hall we blame it on them? In any case, you're not meant to take more than three Topalgique a day. I was soon up to six and more.

I did a couple of blindingly good shows on this stuff. The Paris concert was amazing, and the night before my collapse I did a gig in Rome that was also fantastic. Anita's sister came and her whole family. Dozens of Pallenbergs. Nevertheless it soon became evident that things were getting out of hand. Burning the sheets is always a dead giveaway. Finally, in Milan, I had a seizure and we actually had to cancel the tour. I then proceeded to go cold turkey – cancelling a tour does tend to focus the mind. After a while things got more or less back to normal. But not for long.

———————————

No sooner had I got over this crise than I went down with a kidney infection. The last thing I remember was Cannes – *Marie Antoinette* was up for various awards so I went there with great anticipation. I must have started to get ill. As it turned out Cannes was to be the last thing I remembered for quite a long time. In fact, much of Cannes remains a blur, partly because it all happened in French. I started to get ill with a kidney infection, maybe due to the stress of Cannes. Not to mention taking too many sleeping pills, which were cloaking everything, hiding all the symptoms. My kidneys just couldn't take it any more; they gave out and an opportunistic microbe developed. Doing these festivals is never easy, but not everybody gets a kidney infection from Cannes!

We got home to our flat in Paris and I suddenly found I couldn't walk or go to the loo. François called the doctor and got me into hospital. In Paris it's called Le Centre Réanimation, the reanimation centre – *really* intensive care. Either you come out in a box or you come through by the skin of your teeth. It's assumed you're dying if you go into the place.

And then I went into a coma. It's incredible how easily I can go into a coma. Jesus, that was the scariest thing! Yet another coma! Fucking hell! But I really did the right thing once again, because by going into a coma I avoided the horror, and when I came out, it was all over.

I would come in and out of it and François and I would talk and I promised him (I don't remember doing it) I wouldn't die on him. It wasn't pleasant being in the reanimation centre. They were doing all these strange things to me. It was like being in a torture chamber, actually, but they did save my life. I didn't really know what was happening, I was unconscious and nearly dead, and then they discovered that it was a certain microbe that was going to kill me. Shortly before I went to Cannes I'd had root canal surgery and that might have been the cause of it.

This was my third near-death experience, too many for one person, I'm afraid. But this one was nothing like Australia; you know, seeing Brian Jones's giant face outside my high-rise hotel window. Or even the time I OD'd in Greenwich Village. This time I had a very much simpler journey, where I just thought about the people I loved. I had these experiences of going through time and space, of being able to go anywhere and talk to whoever. I don't exactly know what that was; whether it was people thinking of me and then I would think of them.

One thing I did in these dreams was this psychic crashing – I would crash through ceilings and walls. I would fly through time and space. Time collapse! I had this sense of molecular deconstruction and being weightless, flying around the world in my hospital garb. I saw my loved ones and we sat about and talked. I had long chats with Andrew Oldham and I landed in Dave Courts's sitting room, crashing through the wall in my blue hospital nightie. And I remember thinking, How odd that I can do this and I don't feel any pain! Apart from all the tubes and things, it was just like I was in hospital, and Dave looked up and said: 'Oh, Marianne, you're here! Well, I see you haven't come to do a show.' And it was all like that a bit.

There was one very frightening dream that kept recurring. I was doing a cocaine deal, which I've never done in my life, for a guy who lived in Transylvania. Not a very nice person – they had a bad reputation there in Transylvania, or so it seemed in my dream. I've known some great coke dealers in my day, not everybody who's involved in coke is a cunt, but this guy *was*. And I, in the perverse way I do, had a crush on him. I think I might have even wanted to marry him, but then I don't know who I was being in this dream. I had organised this coke shipment to Transylvania and it arrived, and I thought he'd be very pleased with me, but I must have offended him in some way that I didn't follow. The truth is I never really understand things – even when I'm *not* dreaming. And at that moment when I realised it had all gone wrong somehow he killed me and I killed him. Now you'd think you'd be free of somebody once you'd killed him, but the world turned upside down and we found ourselves locked in a coffin together, looking at each other *for ever*! And I kept having it, again and again, and I began to believe it was true, and then eventually, I heard François say: 'But, Marianne, you've never killed anybody in your life!' And at that moment, it all faded away.

I had some wonderfully baroque dreams, too. There was a bit where I was in Fairyland with the Fairy Queen, like Queen Mab in *Romeo and Juliet*, the fairies' midwife who 'gallops night by night through lovers' brains'. I was a blackbird and we were travelling together through the countryside of England in the sixteenth century and that really was wonderful. I had a lovely time being a blackbird – a Romany blackbird. I could speak. I was it *and* I could watch it.

While I was in a coma I had this dream about Mick and Keith. They were playing in my hospital room. I didn't know if it was on television or if they were actually there in the room. I wasn't feeling too good so I said, 'Look, boys, thank you, I do appreciate it, but I don't really know if I want this right now.' They vanished and I looked up and, projected on the ceiling, there they were, playing some 'Brown Sugar'/'Honky Tonk' kind of song, something with an uptempo rhythm. Maybe a song they haven't written yet!

One of the things I was worrying about when I went into hospital, when I went into the coma, was Keith's head injury after falling out of the palm tree. It kept worrying me in my dreams. I had hallucinations about it, that I was there in the operating room peering into Keith's brain, and it was very scary indeed – the contents of Keith's head! But of course he came out of it just fine. He'll outlive us all.

A few years ago I met up with Keith at the George V Hotel. I remember Keith, in between singing me all these wonderful country love songs, leaning over to me and saying very seriously,

'Now look here: You must never, ever, try to kill yourself.' And
I said, 'What do you mean, man? Why the fuck should I?' And
then I thought about it later and I thought, well, I guess that's
how it must look to him, because I almost lost everything.

———————

The reanimation centre has a very science-fiction sound to it,
but it's really just an intensive care facility. I was out for the
count, but, on the third day, she rose again and asked for a cup
of tea. It's embarrassing to have had such a drama! My friends
said: 'Well, you've always liked a drama! And we know how
actresses love death scenes!'

I was so weak I'd get overcome when I'd have to lift a pen!
And we're talking about contracts! You know it's bad when you
haven't the strength to sign a contract. I'd sign one and initial
every page and then I'd go: 'Oh, no! Not another!' François
looked after me and there you are. What a life!

I came round and started to read to just try and stay alive and
found a really amazing book to disappear into: *Shantaram*. It's a
novel by Gregory David Roberts about an escaped armed robber
who finds redemption through a radiant Bombay street guide, a
sprawling cinemascope epic involving shantytown mystics, war
in Afghanistan and the mystery of love.

Through reading I escaped the painful reality of the
reanimation centre, but the whole incident continued to have an
enormous effect on me – the despair and the disillusionment

were overwhelming. My doctor at the Centre Réanimation said, 'Well, of course, you know what part of the body Galen and Hippocrates associated with disappointment and loss?' And I said, 'No, what?' He said: 'The kidney.'

It had all been very traumatic but François looked after me. I came back from the hospital for the almost dead, not smoking, and having lost ten kilos. It's almost worth a near-death experience to lose ten kilos!

———————

The other day a producer called me from MTV to ask if I'd participate in a documentary on the sexual revolution; I told him he should talk to someone who knows something about it. I don't know where people get this idea that I was a symbolic figure in the hedonistic insurgency of the sixties, like La Marianne in the French Revolution, leading mobs of sexually liberated sans-culottes over the barricades towards indiscriminate drug taking and polymorphous perversity. Sounds good, but it's just not so.

I've given up drugs entirely now. We have said our last goodbyes. Not that I don't now and then think fondly of past highs. I remember quite vividly my first encounter with cocaine. It was the summer of 1967 at a party at the director Christian Marquand's flat. They'd raised the money to make *Candy* and they were celebrating. Robert Fraser laid out six lines of white crystally powder on the table. This was the first time I'd ever seen *lines*. I didn't know what I was meant to do. Robert handed me a rolled-up hundred-dollar bill – the absolutely apropos coke accessory, which Robert *would* have – and handed it to me. 'You *snort* it, darling,' he said helpfully. I followed his instructions, rather too well as it turned out, doing all six lines. Robert's eyes popped out. Coke was a rare and exotic new substance in London – my friend Bill had brought it with him from Rome – but Robert, being a courtly old Etonian, didn't say a thing. Later on I heard he'd told the story to others with the awe generally reserved for Olympic athletes: 'She did all *six lines* – can you believe it?!' It was Merck cocaine, so delicate it was like snowflakes.

Patti Smith once described my generation's promiscuous drug taking as children running through a minefield. But we did have *some* guides. We had Freud, we had Uncle Bill Burroughs. But no one can teach you anything, really; you have to learn these lessons by falling on your face a hundred times. There was Coleridge and De Quincey. 'Thou hast the keys to Paradise, oh just, subtle, and mighty opium!' as De Quincey grandly announced at the beginning of his opium eating, only to end up with 'an Iliad of woes'.

I certainly didn't think I was going to get into smack. I dabbled, I tried it once or twice. Mason Hoffenberg, the poet, wit and savage philosopher who collaborated with Terry Southern on the scandalous novel *Candy*, gave me heroin when I was playing Ophelia, and I threw up every time I went off stage. That was the *real* experience of what happens to the human body when it takes poison. The cure is always in the disease, as Bill Burroughs used to say. That's the whole principle of homeopathic medicine. It cures you by giving you a little bit of the poison.

The people who crossed my path when I was a junkie – Francis Bacon, Brion Gysin, and Kenneth Anger – were all gay men, and, of course, couldn't understand why in the world I wouldn't *want* to live with Mick Jagger! To them, living with Mick Jagger and all that would have been heaven. And for me, too, sometimes it was, but at other times it was hell because I wasn't good at the game. One of the unforeseen consequences of my behaviour was to hurt Mick, which was something I hadn't really gone through at all. I'm ashamed to say, it didn't even occur to me. How that would play with the person I was with – the thought that I would rather go and be a junkie on the street than stay with him? It was such a brutal thing to do.

Brion, Francis, and Kenneth were completely non-judgemental – whether that had anything to do with their being gay, I don't know. They didn't try to stop me, or rescue me, or tell me I was doing the wrong thing, that I was making a big mistake, or any of that shit – and I was grateful to them for that because I really didn't want to hear it. I just wanted to be allowed to do what I wanted to do. If I wanted to live on the fucking wall for two years, then so be it. My plan was to disappear Marianne Faithfull for a while.

Very few people knew who I was. I thought I was invisible, I really did. People would say, well, it doesn't say too much about your other friends that none of them sought you out, but the truth is you couldn't have found me if you'd wanted to. Even the people I knew on the street didn't know my name. They didn't know who I was, or care. But it didn't surprise me at all that Francis Bacon, the man with X-ray eyes, could see me. You had to be an intrepid person to find me. I used to hang out near a pub called The French and Francis would come out, legless, and see me sitting there. We would go to Wheelers and he would feed me. Francis knew a lot about pain, and in a strange way he knew what I was doing. It was something we used to talk about when we were alone, but never in front of anybody else.

I was twenty-three with a needle in my arm. It was as if the lights went out. I was scary-looking, anorexic and incredibly thin, like a skeleton, so if you had come across me you wouldn't have wanted anything to do with me. It was a degrading experience – but apparently not degrading enough! Carrie Fisher explained to me the problem with my life story as the basis for a movie script: it wasn't *bad enough*. I thought I'd degraded myself plenty, but apparently not. I guess I wasn't thinking of the movie rights!

My personal drug guru was Alexander Trocchi, novelist, anarchist, junkie, Lettrist, and, in his essay 'Invisible Insurrection of a Million Minds', theoretician of the spontaneous university. He is most famous for his autobiographical *Cain's Book*, long banned in the UK for its graphic and sympathetic treatment of addiction and promiscuous sex.

I could never shoot myself up; I was really bad at it. I was really bad at being a junkie, actually, so I used to go around to

Alex's and he would do it for me. It was Alex who said, 'This is a terrible way for you to live, Marianne; you have to score your fix every day, and you never have any money. You don't want to end up being a prostitute, which is where you might well find yourself if you keep this up. The best thing to do is go and get registered!' And he was right. The system they had for junkies in those days in England was amazing. That was the beginning of my healing, because suddenly I was being given enough of what I thought of as love; I was given a lot, actually. Dr Willis, the doctor in charge of my case, took a chance on me, and it worked. Thank God I registered as a heroin addict; that saved me, it really did. Dr Willis gave me a prescription for enough heroin every day. I would just go to John Bell & Croyden Chemists and pick it up.

My theory is that heroin substitutes for love, so it makes sense that when you find yourself in a situation without love, you turn to heroin. And then it was like a flash went off in my head. It was like an R. Crumb light bulb came on. And, when I realised that, I went to Dr Willis and said, 'I think I'm ready to come off.' And then began the longest comedown in history . . . eight months of diminution . . . tiny, *tiny* increments, milligram by milligram.

The other thing about heroin is that it spontaneously generates melodramas. OD-ing, trying to score, not scoring, going cold turkey, scaly dealers, ruthless behaviour. And like any melodrama there are plenty of villains – the junkie world is filled with the skuzziest types imaginable. There will always be creepy people around, and before you know it you're in trouble.

At the very point in Bexley Hospital when I had finally got off
heroin entirely, this dreadful geezer showed up wearing a very
fancy dressing gowns and pretending to be a drug addict. I
realised instinctively that he was evil and I left Bexley Hospital
that very day – for India. I figured that was putting enough
distance between me and the Devil's minion. He turned out to
be a journalist from the *News of the World*. What freaked me
out was that, after going through eight months to get *off* drugs,
here was this sleazy guy offering me drugs. What a story that
would have made! MARIANNE FAITHFULL CAUGHT SCORING
DRUGS IN REHAB! Several years later it came out in the paper
that he was a morphine addict and had hanged himself in his
flat.

Unfortunately, I wasn't able to stay off heroin permanently. But
only for the time on the wall did I take it every day – or I
wouldn't be as well as I am now. To get the monkey off my
back took a long time, which I didn't know when I made my
plan. I should have known. It wasn't until I went into treatment
at Hazelden in 1985 that I managed to get off smack completely.

———————————

There's this daft idea – and I know it quite well because I've
told it to myself many times – that the drugs bring out the *real*
you. It's bullshit, of course, and the next day it becomes
painfully obvious, but you still go on doing it.

I used to think one had to have *something*; whatever occasion
you celebrated or if you were depressed, you needed a hit. Or

you needed it to work or go shopping or clean the house – not that I *had* a house or any desire to go shopping in those days, but you know what I mean. Whatever the occasion, it seemed just the thing to get you through it. We were young and didn't know any better. But I turned sixty at the end of last year – time to change.

There's two things I've always thought are interesting: the Romantic image of the artist and its association with the self-inflicted plunge into the abyss of drugs and wretched excess. Which I now happen to think is utter crap. Maybe it worked for De Quincey and Cocteau, and it sounds good when you're fifteen, but ultimately I think it's incredibly immature. It's practically *infantile*. If you're a working artist, you haven't got time for that shit. Which is why Flaubert said the best way to write, to create art, is from a bourgeois life with sleep and food and exercise and all those boring things – and a bit of sex occasionally. You only have to think about Marlon Brando in *Apocalypse Now* to see what a hellish place the Romantic illusion can take you to. It doesn't create anything. It's a supreme form of narcissism.

As far as I'm concerned those overheated Romantic visions of the world are done! I don't want to see things as romantic and doomed and beautiful. In real life, people go through huge problems and deal with them. These young kids in bands who are attracted to smack and crack cocaine and shit are dazzled by images of glamorous decadence. A lot of them, let's face it, really bought into that fascination with the lower depths, what they now call the Old Rock Star's Manual. Where it all ends up – if you analyse it carefully – is with Brando in the cave with a copy of *The Romantic Agony*. What's striking about the horrific situation he finds himself in is that he has never let himself say no to anything. He's simply indulged every urge, every whim. He's not a grand character. He's horrible; he's a monster! That's what happens when you take the Romantic agony or the Romantic ecstasy to its illogical conclusion. Why stop at heroin and crack cocaine? Why not carry on into bestiality and cannibalism and all the rest of it? I think one of the problems is that being an artist is very difficult anyway. It's akin to being a child or reviving childhood. You can see how those two things mesh – childlike invention and childish self-indulgence – but at some point you have to say, I can't live like that any more.

I haven't been passionately self-destructive for about twenty years now. What drives this self-intoxicating behaviour is the adolescent quest to defy conventional morality, to leap over all the petty, mundane things in life into an ecstasy of excess. 'So that you may not be one of the martyred slaves of Time,' as Baudelaire says in '*Enivrez-vous*': 'Get drunk! Get drunk!/and never pause for rest!/With wine, poetry, or virtue,/as you choose!' Or the supreme evocation of anarchic hubris, Rimbaud's *Lettre du voyant*:

> The poet makes himself a seer by a long, deliberate and total disordering of all the senses. All forms of love, suffering, madness: he searches *himself*, he consumes all

the poisons in himself, to keep only their essence . . . He arrives at the unknown, and when, maddened, he ends up by losing the knowledge of his visions: he has still seen them! Let him die charging among those unutterable, unnameable things . . .

This is *fantastic* stuff, it's almost contagious, you get a contact high just reading it, but you have to bear in mind it was written by a teenager – Rimbaud was seventeen at the time. Just the moment in one's life – I should know! – when overweening ideas about transcending everything seem perfectly reasonable and achievable. But I never *quite* fell for all that – though some may think otherwise.

Rimbaud is my idol, but the part I now like best is the bit where he gets to Africa. I like that better than the chaotic travels with Verlaine, although he wrote some great, great poems in that period. But what really interests me is when he becomes absolutely fascinated with reality itself. He never wrote another poem and he got very ill, but ultimately he saw life as it actually is. In the end he inhabited his fantasy world; he went and lived it and at that point felt no need to write about it any more, which, of course, creates other problems. I'm living *my* dream at the moment, and if I didn't need the money, I wouldn't want to *do* anything, either.

There's a lot of reasons why I don't think drugs are a Good Thing, but no matter what I say, people aren't going to take any notice – they'll do what they want. I've done my share, but I've never done as many drugs as people thought I did. Often I didn't have the *money* for smack and coke. Not exactly the most noble motive for resisting drugs, but there you are . . .

———————————

One of the hazards of reforming your evil ways is that some people won't let go of their mind's-eye image of you as a wild thing. If you're not ranting on coke, raving on booze, or legless on Mandrax, you're bound to disappoint fans of your former mad self. I was thinking about that yesterday when dear old Henrietta Moraes came to mind. I remember when she was trying to get clean after a lifetime of drinking. One of the first things that happens when you stop drinking or taking drugs – if you've done them all your life – is that you get physically and mentally depressed; you have no urge to mix or entertain; you can't really think about other people at all, you become very self-centred, withdrawn and quiet. In short, you're no fun to be with.

Monster (David Milinaric), the inspired interior designer, ran into a sober Henrietta and was terribly disappointed to find this subdued person in place of the old hell-raising Hen. 'Oh for God's sake,' he said, 'have a bloody drink, you're so *boring*!' At the time drinking wasn't yet a matter of life and death for Henrietta, but of course eventually it was. She died of cirrhosis.

One thing I've learned is that one shouldn't make stupid pronouncements about giving things up. Like, 'I'm giving up drinking.' It provokes people, for one thing. I just have to take

it one day at a time, but in my case by *not* going to the
meetings. I know many of my friends have saved their lives
by going to AA and NA, but I just can't go back to the rooms.
I can't face it – I'm not prepared to feel that everything I've
done in the last ten years is wrong. I am ready to admit that
my body prefers it when I don't drink, but I'm not sure about
the rest of me! All this trying to give things up can make you
go barking. There's always going to be something that we do
that isn't good for us, but I'm convinced that there's something
in us deep down that needs a break from the regular life. My
theory is that by keeping yourself just *slightly* off the straight
and narrow you can avoid all sorts of things, perhaps *major*
things, that otherwise could spell trouble. I know that when I've
been in top form, off drink and whatever, it's then that I can
get into all sorts of trouble – sexual pickles and all that stuff.
I've even been known to marry the wrong person soon after
sobering up.

Unlike many in my generation I never had that revelation of
the true cosmic nature of the world – or whatever it was people
saw – on psychedelic drugs. I'm sorry, but I just didn't see the
white light. It was a great experience, but it didn't take the
place of my spiritual life. I saw that there were other realities,
but I think I'd always known that. My spiritual life remained
much the same from childhood on, apart from when I was on
heroin – which is one of the best reasons for getting off it. It
kills your inner life.

I recently read Daniel Pinchbeck's *Breaking Open the Head*
about his out-of-body, or should I say out-of-his-mind

experiences on an impressive array of psychedelic dugs. Here was somebody trying to be reasonable about very unreasonable things. But inevitably these psychotropic gurus go off the deep end. There was the late Terence McKenna trying to tell us flying saucers were messengers from the future, and now Pinchbeck is predicting the end of the world. I do think it is going to end, and quite soon, but not because of some goony date in the Mayan calendar – like 2012 – which is Pinchbeck's idea. I think the apocalypse will appear for far more banal reasons than that: war, pestilence, famine, and global warming. And rampant greed. And, of course, sheer incompetence. It ain't gonna get any better. I just hope my grandchildren get to see the world I grew up in and know what a *tree* is. It's tragic, I know. I'm beginning to sound like a complete curmudgeon – but I *am* a curmudgeon! And now I see how curmudgeons get to be that way. This world *sucks*!

I've had as many psychedelic experiences as I need; my head opened, and then I stopped. LSD was a gentle drug for me in that it didn't make me go on and on and on. All it did was open my mind enough to be able to see the not-on-acid reality. Like planting a seed, imagining something and projecting it. Something that starts inside and then slowly grows outward. It's a long-term thing, of course, and you have to be careful because you can end up in some right old snake pits, obviously.

I've been reading a lot of Philip Pullman lately, the *His Dark Materials* trilogy: *The Golden Compass, The Subtle Knife, The Amber Spyglass*. And it reminded me of something I've known my whole life: all these worlds overlap and coexist. That's why it's so easy to reach people, you know, who died. Doorways into different worlds. The danger in all these worlds is the church. What looks like evil is good. And what looks like good is evil, which is the principle of *The Seven Deadly Sins*, and many other things in life, actually. George Bush talking to God and destroying the world. Reading about Oppenheimer, I realised even in something as fundamental as physics there really are different layers of reality. And you can fold them up. String theory. Maybe in our lifetime we'll get to actually see some of them.

As for God – It, Him, Her – I'm a bit Alan-Wattsish that way. *This Is It* or whatever that book was called. We're little chips of God and some of us remember this and some of us don't. It's a great concept, and you find it in all religions. In the Kabbalah it's sparks of light of the Divinity. I think it's one of the few transcendent things you *can* grasp, being yourself a chip off the old cosmic rock.

Drugs like smack don't help you at all; they cut all that out. While I was on smack I lost my connection to the cosmos, but eventually I got it back, thank God! I'm sorry, but I don't believe in a Creator, I don't believe I was made by some outside Being. I follow the Darwinian principle. However, I do believe there's a divine spark in everybody where all art and beauty and truth come from and it's our job to uncover that – and the ability to tend your own garden. I'm getting to the point where I literally want to tend my own garden. It's very Brit, that desire to get your hands in dirt and plant something, although I don't think I'm actually going to get my hands all that dirty. Gloves, perhaps – or maybe I'll hire a gardener!

_____

'A cigarette is the perfect type of a perfect pleasure,' as Oscar Wilde so aptly put it. 'It is exquisite, and leaves one unsatisfied. What more can one want?' And that made me think about how one unsatisfactory indulgence can lead to another – the insidious interdependency of drugs. Sleep and smoking – that's really where it all came from. That's why it was so important I stopped smoking. One of the things that got me into such a *mania* with the sleeping pills in the first place. I couldn't sleep and when I couldn't sleep, I smoked. That train of events: I must sleep, I must sleep, and if I can't sleep, I'll smoke. François and I used to smoke when we'd wake up in the middle of the night. We'd light a cigarette – me in my bed, and François walking around; he'd get up and light a cigarette, and now we don't. So that's all going to be much better for my voice, but now there's still the problem of what to do when I wake up in the middle of the night. Eat!

I can't handle anything that's going to hurt my work. That's what's really frightening to me, the thought of going on stage and not being able to sing. I have on occasion been on stage drunk, but not for years, not since I was stupid that time in Ireland. I don't get drunk any more, but, unfortunately, what I did do when I first stopped drinking was *smoke* my brains out, and for a singer that's about the worst thing you can do. When you're addicted to something, health seems rather an abstract concept, but you do expect when you give it up for your body to say, *merci bien*, well done! But as soon as I stopped smoking, I caught the mother of all colds. That's what happens: you reform, you give up your bad habits – and, fucking hell, you get sick! It's your body cleaning itself of the poison. You want to be rewarded immediately for your piety, your saintly abstinence but it's *months* before you start to feel really good.

Oh God, the agony of quitting! I remember once, in Boston again, I stopped smoking for four days and I got so high, but not connected to anything, not tied down. I got very light, and I got really scared that I was never going to be an intense person again – which is crap, actually, because I'm exactly the same as I ever was. I just feel a bit more detached. I think that drugs are part of the way we connect to ourselves. What John Lennon said about smoking was that it helped to tie him down to earth, and I always believed that.

Sometimes it feels like my whole life for the last two years has been about not smoking. Unless I was touring, I always tried to come home early. I didn't want to get drunk, because I knew if I did I'd definitely smoke too much. So, no more bad habits. As long as I don't get drunk or take drugs or smoke, I'll be all right. And I've got to be careful what I eat, of course, but I'm being very careful, because when you stop smoking you tend to put on weight. Ach, it's endless!

I don't feel quite as involved in things without a cigarette, without my prop, but there's nothing to be done about it. The thing about not smoking is I'm breathing so much better.

I think if I'd gone on smoking, I would have got really ill, because I was *wheezing* like an old organ (and we don't want that!). It's interesting to go out to lunch just to see how you do. I don't feel envious of the people smoking. François still does, that's why he needs his fake cigarette, because his image of himself is very much with a cigarette. He's got a cigarette in a holder which has a mint taste to it to stop him from wanting to smoke. He's having a much harder time of it than I did. He's in his suit with a fake cigarette clamped towards his face, and his glasses, and he looks *exactly* like Groucho.

I had a long chat with Anita the other day, talking about how destructive it is at our age to be smoking. Yoko stopped. She just decided to stop and did it. Smoking, my last self-destructive act. Since I've turned sixty, I've realised I've really got to watch it. I never expected to turn sixty, you know. I've come to believe like Nietzsche that things *do* come back. But, dear returning gyre, leave me alone, please, leave me as I am.

I was just starting yesterday to read a wonderful John Cooper Powys novel and I found myself pondering – and not understanding at all a Latin quotation in it. It bothered me dreadfully that I couldn't translate it. 'After Shakespeare and Milton,' Powys writes, 'my favourite poet is Horace. And I rejoice to think how much I owe to his special use of that splendid word *"impavidum"* which comes in so grandly at the close of one of his very noblest of all poems: *"Si fractus illabatur orbis impavidum serient ruinae".*' I finally found a friend of mine who remembered a bit of his classical education and he translated it for me. It's from Book III of Horace's *Odes*. It goes:

'Even if the broken orb of the Universe falls into collapse I'll remain undaunted.' It's a little like Jimi Hendrix's 'If the mountains fell in the sea/Let it be, it ain't me . . . If all the hippies cut off all their hair/Oh, I don't care.' And I guess that's the way I feel – a little naked without all my props and habits – but *undaunted*, goddammit!

Some of us do drugs *and* make records, some of us just make records or tour or work, because as we get older we can't really indulge in all those fun bad things. I wish we could. I wish I was Cocteau! I wish I could be sitting in the Deux Magots with all the bad boys of literature and art, sipping a glass of absinthe and throwing off grand Existential *mots* like Cocteau:

> Everything one does in life, even love, occurs in an express train racing toward death. To smoke opium is to get out of the train while it is still moving. It is to concern oneself with something other than life or death.

Don't worry, there's nothing to say. I'll cope. I've come through worse! I'm probably a bit high on the natch, as the old hipsters used to say – a lot *they* knew about that. When something changes that drastically in one's life you get a big rush of adrenaline from it. Well, man, that's the way the cookie crumbles. Or, as they say in Latin: *Sic transit gloria mundi* – and that's about the only Latin I know!

i join the club

Cancer. Does anyone ever think it's going to happen to them?
It's always someone else until one day it's not. Funny, when
close friends become ill you try to put yourself in their place.
But you don't know what a bad job you've done until the day
that insidious, unwanted guest comes to call on you.

I had my first inkling that something was wrong last summer.
Feeling a little unwell, that sort of thing. The year leading up to
my cancer had been so hard, physically and psychically, that I
wonder if my body didn't know all along that something was
wrong.

The year had been a series of disasters, the last one being my
kidney infection. I'd supposedly recovered, but I still didn't feel
completely well. I was about to go on tour when it happened: I
found a lump. Just a little lump. It practically takes your breath
away. Followed by a whirlwind of emotions: fear, of course, but
also resignation, curiosity, anger, and even, yes, a strange elation
(in a when-you-got-nothing-you-have-nothing-to-lose way).
Then, suddenly, you find yourself in a doctor's office. How you

got there, you have no idea. The doctor was incredibly handsome, late sixties, very tall, and with the most wonderful slightly red nose, the sort of nose you get from drinking too much good claret. There's a French name for it, a nez rosé, I think it is.

'How long is it since you've had a mammogram?' he asked. I could barely look him in the eye. Let's just say it had been a while.

Funnily enough, the lump I felt was not cancer, but at the same time they found something right inside at the back. Just a little, tiny thing, so small it was hard to believe how dangerous it was. Of course it all had to come out. This little area, you see, was plotting on making a tumour! It's really a fiendish thing. The thing was so tiny they had to have a special X-ray blown up hugely so the doctor could even see it. And because the thing was so small, it was a very complicated operation. My doctor, thank God, was a great diagnostician; another doctor might have missed it. And it was fortunate that all this happened in Paris, because Paris is cancer central. In fact, when I was growing up, people who got cancer usually died. The kind of treatment I got just didn't exist back then.

François and I really did completely flip when the cancer was found. François went on a four-day tear; I just sat here in my apartment in Paris thinking, 'Oh fuck! What about my garden? And the Arabian quarter horse I'm gonna buy some day?' But François really pulled himself together after his little drinking bout and he's been an absolute star. As for me, well, you'd have to ask François. Hopefully, I haven't been the worst patient in the world.

I'm not exactly proud of my first reaction when I heard I had cancer: sheer panic, really scared. I didn't know what to think, much less how to act. Whether to just pretend everything was all right or what. I did try to stay calm, and I told myself I was really lucky it had been detected so early. Basically, I just left it to the doctors. I put myself in their hands – which can turn out quite badly sometimes, too. I guess I was also lucky in that department.

Just to show you how mad I am, I said to the surgeon, 'But can't I do the tour and then have the operation?'

He looked at me incredulously and said, 'Well, of course, you *could* do that, but haven't you ever heard, cancer cells are splitting as we speak; they are spreading exponentially. With the stress of the tour, by the time you get back, it will be really bad.' So we had to put the tour off and I had to deal with it straight away, which was very frightening. There's a certain part of my personality where things just don't go into my brain.

'No,' my doctor said, 'you go into hospital *next* week.'

Even though I had cancelled the tour and opted for immediate surgery, from the time of the detection until the operation felt like a very long wait. I went through a period of great depression just waiting to hear the results. Having to cancel the tour was really sad and difficult. And then there was François thinking I was going to die! Me not knowing whether I was going to die! Wondering whether perhaps I wanted to. Hmm, that would have been convenient, but unfortunately just then I decided I didn't want to. Die. Human nature, I guess.

I was very lucky. I didn't have to have chemotherapy, I didn't have to have radiotherapy. So what happened was that I had six months off. I did nothing really. I just went for my little walks in the Tuileries. I went to Ireland; I went to see my friends.

I have so many friends who've died of cancer. Cancer is cancer and cancer is everywhere. I think if you're a young person and get cancer your reaction is 'I've got to fight, I've got to battle', but, as far as cancer is concerned, I felt the very opposite: 'Surrender, accept that whatever will happen will happen.' And some very weird things did happen. For example, as I was coming around from the operation the nurse realised there was a haematoma, which is an internal bruise and very dangerous. So they had to put me under again and take it out, which was a real nightmare.

Everybody's been impossibly there for me. It's something I have to remind myself about and be thankful for. My dear old friend Cynthia Fitzgerald called me. Jeremy Clyde – of Chad & Jeremy ('Yesterday's Gone', etc.), and an old lover of mine – sent me a lovely note that said, 'I read the news today, oh boy!' I got the most wonderful letter from my old boyfriend and bass player Ben Brierly saying he'd heard I was ill and was glad to hear I was now okay; he offered me a lovely little house he has with servants for a vacation in the sun. Oliver Musker rang me from India. We all have our different lives but are still fond of each other. Gus Van Sant sent flowers. Anita calls me once a week just to see how I am. Chris Blackwell's been so good. Paul and Cathy McGuinness have been wonderful. Dave Courts and John Dunbar just great. Also got a lovely message from Yoko.

Mick called. Keith sent some great faxes (with drawings of pirates):

> Dear Marianne. Got your message. Many thanks and the same to you. 60's got nothing, try 63!! You're damn right about the comedown after a big tour, but it's par for the course. Glad to hear you'll soon be back in harness. Heigh-ho! Will be in Europe. Right now languishing on the beach drinking Bushwackers and a variety of exotic concoctions. I send you one love, Keith. Love, love Patty.

I'm sure we'll see 'Heigh-ho!' in a song soon.

Everybody rallied. Daniel de la Falaise gave me all these books on how to eat properly against cancer. That's all very important. Marsha Hunt, singer, actress, novelist and Mick's one-time squeeze, gave me her book *Undefeated* in which she explains how she decided to treat her cancer as an opportunity to transform perceptions of female sexuality and beauty. I haven't lost my sex appeal, thank God. I feel sexy, anyway. And the fact that my breasts are a bit smaller is not such a bad thing – they're not so heavy. I never liked that 'angel with big tits' business as it was. Anyway, they're not *that much* smaller.

Marsha was really wonderful. She sent me a very nice letter and became my cancer buddy.

Anything that affects your breasts naturally strikes deeply at your femininity and sexuality. Maybe I'll mind more later, but at the moment I'm just so glad to be alive. Of course, it's not quite over yet. I have to massage my breasts every morning and every evening to keep them hydrated so that I can slowly massage them back into the right shape. The scars will fade. They're almost faded now actually.

I was very fortunate. And let me tell you, it does wonders for the bitterness one feels about the past. In fact, it's gone! One of the more interesting consequences is how connected to people I feel. I feel much more a part of everything. I've been talking to Hazel, my half-sister, again, and we had not been close in recent years.

I went to see my son Nicholas and got to know his new wife, Teresa. If it took all this for us to get closer to Nicholas again, it was in some way worth it. During his first marriage, things were fraught between us – I lost him.

I don't think Nicholas realised until I got the kidney infection and almost died how precious the connection is. It was then that he began to think, 'Oh fuck, I might lose her. And there's so much more to say!' He had such a hard time of it when he was little. He was taken away from me. We need to use the time we've got left together.

With the onset of cancer I realised that I just had to surrender to the process. We're all going to die and whether your cancer is malignant or goes into remission, everybody who has cancer has to face it. With luck we may get some more time, but cancer is a chronic condition, and once you've had it, you're on the list, because it can come back – and often does.

When you have a serious illness the business of one's mortality looms up. To be honest, it's been on my mind for ages. The other day when I listened to 'Like Being Born', the song I wrote with Beck, which has the line 'my father promised me roses', I realised that my songs are often an odd mixture of love and death. Even at eighteen, I was 'in love with easeful death'. Like many young people I could indulge in morbid fantasies. From my reading, my Romantic agony, I thought that death was the next great adventure, but I don't think that any more. And now I don't see that I have any choice.

So I'm somewhat sorry to say I've given up most of my bad habits and even taken up some good ones. Don't get me wrong, I haven't become a health nut. But the connection between my health and doing my work – you've got to at least be *alive* to do it! – has suddenly become (scarily) obvious to me.

You see, it has occurred to me that, now that I'm sixty, it might be a good time to start taking care of myself (and none too soon). After all, it's never too late. Or so I keep telling myself.

they'll never make a saint of me either

Behind the façade and the drugs – when I did take them, that is! – I'm a snake pit of fears and insecurities. Depression, addiction, crippling stage fright, masses of guilt – which in the past only spurred me on to more self-destructive behaviour. Turning my demons into my magical helpers hasn't always been easy; it took huge amounts of psychic energy. I just started reading Peter Carey's *My Life as a Fake* and it awakened several nasty little demons. I'm constantly terrified I'm going to be exposed as a fraud. My paranoia about it is a bit insane, really because, at the same time, I'm working with François on the box set of my music and, bugger me, if there's one thing my life has not been, it's a fake. But it's so odd that I still have that feeling. Perhaps it has something to do with my inability to grow up. It's sometimes seen as a charming, childlike quality from the sixties, but it has actually made my life very hard and complicated, and dismayed my long-suffering friends and lovers.

I do have this yearning to be a good person. Not that I was ever a *bad* person, really – or at least I didn't mean to be. A bad *girl*, maybe. But, honestly, if one wants to multiply one's problems of existing as a person on this earth, just add drugs and fame – it's amazing that anybody behaves with any decency at all! Not many of us do, actually. I'm not trying to be a saint – like Allen so wanted – I'm just glad I've grown slightly less intolerant of people. I can be somebody still striving towards trying to love people and forgive people. I don't have to be a sort of absolute horror.

enormous plans at the last minute

Sometimes I wonder if I'm not turning into my mother. Honestly, I like to be in bed, smoking a sneaky cigarette and drinking a cup of tea. I know I'm coming up on a tour, so I'm not going to be able to sit in this lovely room reading John Updike and watching *M.A.S.H.* for quite a long time.

Leonard Cohen came up with something recently I was delighted to hear. He said it's a scientific fact – I always like bits of information that begin like that, especially from a Buddhist monk! – as you get older, the cells that produce anxiety just fade away. And he's nearly eighty, so he should know. I'm not quite there yet, but it's something to look forward to! Especially in my case, my past being strewn with pratfalls, faux pas, and debacles.

The last time I saw Dave van Ronk, the mayor of McDougal Street, he sang, 'You been a good old wagon, daddy, but you done broke down'. And then, in that wheezy, rusty voice of his, he said, 'I used to think this was a funny song, but now when I get to my age, I don't think it's so funny any more!' And now *I* know what he means.

There are drawbacks to reflecting on the past, but if you live long enough, you inevitably run into it. Earlier this year I went to stay with Sally Henzell in Jamaica after her husband Perry Henzell, director of *The Harder They Come,* died of leukaemia. It was then I realised what it's like to lose your soul mate. People say love is for ever, but is life for ever? Is *anything* for ever? What can you say? So what I'm thinking now is, Oh my fucking Christ! It looks like I may be around for another twenty years. I better save some money.

index